30-Minute

Vegetarian
Indian

Cookbook

Other titles in The 30-Minute Vegetarian Series

30-Minute Vegetarian Mexican Cookbook

30-Minute Vegetarian Thai Cookbook (Fall/Winter 1998–99)

30-Minute

Vegetarian
Indian

Cookbook

Mridula Baljekar

THE ECCO PRESS

THE ECCO PRESS
100 West Broad Street
Hopewell, New Jersey 08525

Printed in the United States of America

Library of Congress Cataloging-in-Publication Data

Baljekar , Mridula.
30-minute vegetarian Indian cookbook / Mridula Baljekar.— 1st Ecco ed.
p.   cm.
Includes Index.
ISBN 0-88001-600-0
1. Vegetarian cookery.   2. Cookery , Indian   3. Quick and Easy
cookery.   I. Title.
TX837.B258   1998
641.5'636'0954—dc21   97-51604

Designed by Typeworks
The text of this book is set in Spectrum
9 8 7 6 5 4 3 2 1
FIRST EDITION 1998

Dedicated to my late mother-in-law,
Shanta Baljekar,
whose creativity and speed always amazed me.
A vegetarian all her life,
it was her excellent cooking
which prompted me to experiment
with vegetarian recipes.

Contents

Introduction

Cooking Indian dishes is usually thought to be time-consuming, with lengthy preparation of ingredients and the numerous spices needed.

I agree!

There is nothing like cooking in the traditional way if you are able to devote the time and effort to it, and sharing an appetizing and nourishing meal with family and friends is something we all enjoy. I have always believed that good food is an essential part of a happy life: it not only nourishes the body, it also nourishes the mind.

Cooking good food does not necessarily have to involve buying expensive ingredients and spending a great deal of time on elaborate preparation and cooking methods. Most of us lead busy lives that prevent us from devoting much time to cooking, but, with a little imagination and care, fast yet delicious meals can be created with minimal effort. I am continuously trying to minimize the work involved in traditional cooking without sacrificing quality or taste,

and you will see how well I have succeeded later.

Indian spices have a magical power to transform humble ingredients into something quite exciting. It is hardly surprising that Western countries were lured to India by the mystique of its spices. To any Indian, they reflect good taste, and using the splendor of the spices well is what Indian cooking is all about. You do not need the entire range of spices to cook quick, tasty, everyday meals. Using just a few basic ones means you can create an amazing variety of flavors. Combining these spices in the correct proportions is the very essence of Indian cooking, and the variety of possible combinations means you can create just the right flavor for your chosen dish. Using different cooking techniques makes for even more variations. Just follow the instructions and you will not be disappointed (I promise!). Once you have mastered the art of cooking quick Indian dishes, which should not take you very long, you will feel confident enough to experiment with your own combinations of spices.

All the recipes in this book are quick and simple, using ingredients that are readily available. The large supermarkets now have a dazzling array of ingredients from around the world, and you can go to specialty food shops, too, if you like. Once you have equipped your pantry, you are ready to cook a speedy meal.

Before you make a start on any dish, have a quick glance at the slow cooking or simmering times in the recipe. You will save time by using these times to prepare the ingredients for another or other dishes. Simple things like boiling water in a kettle rather than waiting for it to boil in a saucepan will save time, too. Also, using hot or warm water helps to enhance the flavors of the spices—adding cold water to carefully blended spices actually impairs their taste.

I have created the recipes in this book with great care, ensuring that the following three points apply to each one:

- they have a speedy cooking time
- they are easy to prepare
- they are tasty and nourishing.

In compiling these recipes my aim has been to show you how to cook traditional dishes that are delicious and exciting but which are quick to make. I have personally cooked every recipe in this book and worked out all the short-cuts without sacrificing taste so that you can make an entire menu in only 30 minutes!

This is possible because not every Indian dish takes a long time to prepare and cook—we have numerous dishes that can easily fit into a 30-minute schedule. Here are just a few examples.

In India we thrive on lentils and have a dazzling variety of them. They are one of the main sources of protein in our diet, and they cook in 30 minutes, most of which is simmering time. This allows you time to cook one of the staples (potato, rice, bread) and a side dish.

Dried beans and peas, which are widely used in Indian cooking, are also excellent sources of protein and dietary fiber. If you soak them the previous night or in the morning, you can cook them very quickly in a pressure cooker. Canned beans and peas also work very well—just drain and rinse them thoroughly. Chickpeas, red kidney beans, black-eyed beans and so on hold their shape and absorb the flavors of the spices very well. I succumb to these every time!

Having only 30 minutes for each meal, it is not easy to make traditional Indian breads, but we are lucky to be able to buy a wonderful range of breads in most supermarkets these days. You will find tips and hints on efficient ways to reheat supermarket breads as well as how you can turn them into something really exotic!

Rice is easy to fit into a 30-minute schedule. Basmati rice cooks in just 8 to 10 minutes if you soak it first for 30 minutes. But do not despair—although 30 minutes is better, you can get away with 15! Then there is easy-cook basmati rice, which is the answer to every frantic cook's prayers. There are several recipes in the book that use this rice.

In some cases, I have used potato as the staple instead of the traditional rice and bread. I think it is much more fun to be inventive in the kitchen. If you like what you have cooked, why worry about tradition?

How about a spicy vegetarian burger with Indian-style French fries?

As far as vegetables are concerned, frozen are just as good as fresh, and they save on preparation time. You can use fresh vegetables to make interesting and wholesome salads—with a touch of spice. These make lovely side dishes, saving you the time you would have needed to cook the vegetables.

The pantry

All you need to do now is equip your pantry. One trip to a good supermarket or an Indian shop will prepare you to rustle up quick and delicious meals for months. In the following pages you will find lists of those ingredients that I recommend you keep in your cupboard.

STANDARD WHOLE SPICES, which should be stored in air-tight jars, away from direct light:

- black mustard seeds
- black cumin seeds (shahi jeera)
- cumin seeds
- coriander seeds
- fenugreek seeds

- fennel seeds
- whole black peppercorns
- bay leaves
- curry leaves (available dried and fresh—fresh ones can be frozen and used straight from the freezer)
- dried red chilies (small ones and long slim ones)
- cassia bark or cinnamon sticks
- whole cloves
- green cardamom pods
- poppy seeds—cream-colored rather than black
- sesame seeds

STANDARD GROUND SPICES, which should be stored in the same way as whole spices:

- turmeric
- coriander
- cumin
- garam masala
- chili powder
- paprika
- asafoetida

STANDARD FRESH INGREDIENTS:

- onions
- garlic—store in a cool, dry place, ideally with the potatoes
- gingerroot—store it like garlic
- fresh green chilies—buy a small number of them and store in the fridge, where they will keep for 3 to 4 weeks if you remove the stalks and store them in a screw-top jar, or wash and freeze them and use frozen

To keep fresh coriander, immerse the roots in a jar of water—it will then keep for 6 to 7 days. To preserve it for 2 weeks or more, wrap the roots with a damp cloth and put the bunch of coriander in a large plastic food bag, root side down. Tie up the bag loosely, making sure no air is trapped, then store the bag in the salad drawer of your fridge. Alternatively, remove the roots, wash and chop the leaves and freeze them. They can then be used frozen.

DRY INGREDIENTS:
- masoor dhal—split red lentils
- moong dhal—skinned and split mung beans
- chickpeas (garbanzos)—buy these only if you would rather soak and precook them; otherwise, buy cans of beans
- black-eyed beans—buy these only if you would rather soak and precook them; otherwise, buy cans of beans
- red kidney beans—buy these only if you would rather soak and precook them; otherwise, buy cans of beans
- lima beans—buy these only if you would rather soak and precook them; otherwise, buy cans of beans
- basmati rice
- easy-cook basmati rice
- ground rice
- besan—gram or chickpea flour

CANNED GOODS:
- chopped tomatoes
- chickpeas (garbanzos)

- lima beans
- black-eyed beans
- red kidney beans
- coconut milk

MISCELLANEOUS ITEMS:
- tomato purée
- crushed tomatoes
- coconut milk powder
- creamed coconut
- shredded coconut
- tamarind concentrate or tamarind juice
- ghee—clarified butter (see note page 67)
- sunflower or soya oil
- Rooh Afza—rose-flavored syrup
- rose water

If you have trouble finding any of these ingredients in your area, many are available by mail order from Kalustyan's, 123 Lexington Avenue, New York, NY 10016, tel. (212) 685-3451, fax (212) 683-8458.

30-Minute

Vegetarian Indian

Cookbook

Soups and Snacks

In India, serving soup as a first course is not at all common. Generally, it is served as an appetizer or as an accompaniment to a meal. In southern India, some soups are used to moisten rice in a meal.

As well as recipes that are ideal for the traditional Indian role for soups, you will find here some soups that can be served as a meal if you combine them with a light snack. I would go even further to minimize work and serve them with a selection of bought Indian breads—delicious!

India is a nation of snack lovers. This is evident from the enormous range available from every corner shop and street vendor in India. We have snacks to suit all moods and occasions. Sometimes we even quite effortlessly make up an entire meal from snacks!

Here you will find some familiar and some unusual snacks, all of which are easy, quick and delicious.

Soups and snacks together can make a fun meal—one I find quite irresistible.

Lemon and Lentil Soup

Serves 4

Adelicious soup based on a hot South Indian recipe known as Rasam. I am not a great fan of very hot food, so this version is rather mild.

Serve with Chili and Coriander Toast or Cheese and Coriander Baguettes (pages 21 and 22).

15-oz can lentil soup
½ teaspoon salt, or to taste
2½ cups water
1–2 whole fresh green chilies
1 tablespoon dried or ½ tablespoon fresh curry leaves
1 teaspoon cumin seeds

½ teaspoon black peppercorns
1 tablespoon sunflower or soya
   oil
½ teaspoon black mustard seeds
¼ teaspoon asafoetida
1 tablespoon lemon juice

1) Put the soup into a saucepan and add the salt, water, chilies and curry leaves. Place over medium heat and gradually bring to a boil.

2) Meanwhile, put the cumin seeds and the peppercorns together in a plastic storage bag and crush them lightly. Add this mixture to the soup. When the soup begins to boil, reduce the heat and simmer gently, uncovered, for 10 minutes.

3) Strain the soup and push down some of the spices that remain in the strainer with the back of a spoon so that all the juices are extracted from them. Set aside.

4) Heat the oil in a small saucepan until it is almost smoking. Remove the pan from the heat and add the mustard seeds, following quickly with the asafoetida. Pour the seasoned oil into the soup, add the lemon juice and serve with the suggested breads.

Hearty Vegetable Soup

Serves 4

✧

A wonderfully satisfying main course soup that will take you no more than 20 minutes to make. Serve with some delicious Cheese and Coriander Baguettes (page 22).

¼ cup butter

1 small onion, finely chopped

2 large garlic cloves

½–1 teaspoon salt, or to taste

1 cup finely chopped potatoes

1 cup finely chopped carrots

1 cup finely chopped green
   beans

scant 2 cups hot water

2 vegetable stock (bouillon)
   cubes

1 cup frozen or canned,
   drained sweet corn

1¼ cups milk

1 teaspoon ground cumin

½ teaspoon ground nutmeg

½ teaspoon freshly ground
   black pepper

1 tablespoon cornstarch,
   blended with a little water

½ cup heavy cream

1) Reserving 1 tablespoon butter, in a large saucepan melt the remainder gently over medium-low heat and cook the onion in it for 2–3 minutes.

2) Meanwhile, crush the garlic cloves with a pestle or the back of a wooden spoon. Discard the skin and crush the cloves together with the salt until you have a fine pulp. Add this to the onion and cook for 2–3 minutes.

3) Add the potatoes, carrots and beans. Cook for 2–3 minutes, then add the water and crumble in the stock cubes. Bring to a boil, cover and reduce the heat. Simmer gently for 15 minutes.

4) Add the sweet corn and milk. Bring back to a boil, reduce the heat, cover and simmer for 5 minutes.

5) Melt the reserved 1 tablespoon butter in a small saucepan over low heat. When it stops sizzling, stir in the cumin, nutmeg and pepper. Let them sizzle gently for 15–20 seconds then stir into the soup.

6) Add the blended cornstarch and cream. Simmer for 1–2 minutes, remove from the heat and serve sprinkled with more freshly ground black pepper, if desired.

Fresh Coriander Soup

Serves 4

1 cup chopped fresh coriander, with stalks

1¼ cups grated potatoes

1 cup chopped fresh or canned tomatoes

3¾ cups hot water

1 teaspoon ground cumin

½ teaspoon freshly ground black pepper

1 teaspoon salt, or to taste

1 tablespoon sunflower or soya oil

½ teaspoon black mustard seeds

6 fenugreek seeds

1) Put the coriander, potatoes and tomatoes into a saucepan and add the hot water. Bring to a boil, then add the cumin, pepper and salt. Reduce the heat, cover and simmer gently for 10 minutes.

2) Strain the soup and push as much of the pulp as possible through the strainer. When you are left with only a dry mixture in the strainer, discard it.

3) Heat the oil in a small saucepan over medium heat. When it is quite hot, but not smoking, throw in the mustard seeds. As soon as they start popping, remove the pan from the heat and add the fenugreek seeds. Let the seeds sizzle for 10–15 seconds, then pour them over the soup. Stir and serve.

Tomato and Coriander Soup

Serves 4

*B*ased on a recipe from southern India, this soup is served in a cup to accompany a meal.

2 tablespoons sunflower or soya oil	12–14 dried curry leaves
2 garlic cloves, crushed	2½ cups chopped fresh or canned tomatoes
½-inch cube gingerroot, peeled and grated	1¼ cups hot water
2 dried red chilies, chopped	1 teaspoon salt
½ teaspoon black peppercorns, crushed	1 teaspoon sugar
	1 tablespoon chopped fresh coriander

1) In a saucepan heat the oil and cook the garlic, ginger, chilies, peppercorns and curry leaves until the garlic and ginger have browned and the chilies have blackened a little.
2) Add the tomatoes and pour in the hot water.
3) Add the salt and sugar and bring to a boil. Cover and simmer for 15–20 minutes. Then let it cool slightly before blending it in a blender and straining it.
4) Return the soup to the saucepan and reheat gently. Stir in the coriander leaves and serve.

Vermicelli and Vegetable Soup

Serves 4

*T*his is a main meal soup with delicate spicing. Serve with any of the snacks given later in this section or just a hot roll and butter if you prefer.

1 cup plain vermicelli
¼ cup butter
2 garlic cloves, chopped
½ teaspoon salt, or to taste
1 medium onion, finely
   chopped
½ cup cubed carrots
1 cup cubed potatoes
2½ cups hot water
½ cup frozen peas
½ cup frozen or canned,
   drained sweet corn

1¼ cups milk
⅔ cup light cream
1½ tablespoons cornstarch,
   blended with a little water
1½ teaspoons ground cumin
½ teaspoon ground coriander
½ teaspoon crushed black
   peppercorns
1 tablespoon finely chopped
   fresh coriander

1) Break up the clusters of vermicelli and put them into a saucepan of boiling water. Boil for 1 minute, then drain off the water, rinse thoroughly in cold water and leave to drain.

2) Reserve 2 tablespoons of the butter and in a saucepan melt the remaining butter gently. Crush the garlic to a smooth pulp together with the salt and cook with the onion for 4–5 minutes, or until soft.

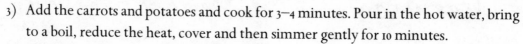

3) Add the carrots and potatoes and cook for 3–4 minutes. Pour in the hot water, bring to a boil, reduce the heat, cover and then simmer gently for 10 minutes.

4) Add the peas, sweet corn and milk. Bring back to a boil, then cook, uncovered, over medium heat for 5 minutes.

5) Add the cream, vermicelli and blended cornstarch. Cook for a further 3–4 minutes.

6) In a small saucepan, meanwhile, melt the remaining butter. When the foam subsides, take the pan off the heat and add the spices. Let them sizzle gently for 15–20 seconds, then pour the spiced butter over the soup. Stir and cook for 1–2 minutes, then add the coriander and serve.

Lentil and Vegetable Soup

Serves 4

A delicious and sustaining, warming soup—ideal for a winter's evening. Serve it with a snack such as Bread Pakoras or Chili and Coriander Toast (pages 19 and 21) or just hot rolls and butter.

I have used tamarind juice to give the soup a hint of tanginess. Make sure it is tamarind juice and not the concentrated paste you use as the paste will make the soup too sour-tasting and darken the color. Alternatively, you could use lime juice if you wish.

2 tablespoons ghee or butter
1 teaspoon coriander seeds
1 teaspoon cumin seeds
½ teaspoon whole black
   peppercorns
2 long, slim, dried red chilies,
   chopped
¼ teaspoon fenugreek seeds
3 large garlic cloves, crushed
15 dried curry leaves
½ teaspoon ground turmeric
¼ cup dried split red lentils
   (masoor dhal)

3¾ cups hot water
1 cup finely chopped green
   beans
2 cups finely chopped green
   cabbage
1 cup very small cauliflower
   florets
1 teaspoon salt, or to taste
1 tablespoon tamarind juice
   (not paste, see above)

1) In a saucepan heat the ghee or butter over medium heat. When it is hot, remove the pan from the heat and add all the ingredients except the lentils, hot water,

vegetables, salt, and tamarind juice. Return the pan to low heat and cook the ingredients gently for 1 minute.

2) Add the lentils and, over medium heat, stir-fry the mixture for 1 minute.

3) Pour in the hot water. Bring to a boil, reduce the heat to low, cover the pan and simmer very gently for 20 minutes.

4) In a blender, purée the soup and strain it into the rinsed-out saucepan. Now add the green beans and cook, covered, over a medium heat for 3–4 minutes.

5) Add the cabbage and cook, covered, for 3–4 minutes.

6) Add the cauliflower, cover and cook for 2–3 minutes.

7) Add the salt and tamarind juice, stir, then simmer for 2–3 minutes before removing the pan from the heat and serving.

Eggplant Fritters

Serves 4

*T*raditionally, eggplant slices are salted and left to drain before cooking, but I have found that this is not really necessary. In this recipe the slices are soaked in salted water prior to cooking just to prevent them from discoloring while you are getting the other ingredients ready—not salting them makes no difference to the flavor or bitterness in the skin.

Serve with Lemon and Lentil Soup and Cumin and Coriander Bread (pages 4 and 136). You can also serve these as a side dish with rice and any dhal or roll. Otherwise, two or three in a chapatti make a filling snack.

2 eggplants, about 1 lb total
1 teaspoon salt, or to taste
2 teaspoons ground cumin
1 teaspoon ground coriander
1 teaspoon onions seeds
  (kalonji)
½ teaspoon aniseed or fennel
  seeds
1½ cups gram flour (besan)

½ cup ground rice or rice flour
1¼ cups cold water
oil, for deep-frying
½ oz fresh coriander leaves or
  fresh mint leaves
1½ tablespoons chili sauce
1 teaspoon bottled minced
  green chilies, optional

1) Slice the eggplants into ¼-inch thick rounds, put them into a bowl of salted water and leave to soak until you are ready.

2) Mix all the spices together in a mixing bowl and sift the besan over them. Add the ground rice or rice flour and mix well. Gradually add the cold water, mixing it in, until you have a batter of coating consistency.

3) Drain the eggplant slices and pat dry.

4) Meanwhile, start heating the oil in a deep frying pan or wok over medium heat.

5) Also, chop the coriander or mint finely and mix them into the chili sauce, adding the minced chilies, if using, and ¼ teaspoon salt. Spread about ¼ teaspoon of this mixture onto a slice of eggplant and cover with another slice to make a sandwich. Dip the "sandwich" into the spiced batter, making sure it is fully coated and is holding firmly together. Put as many "sandwiches" as you can into the hot oil without overcrowding the pan. Fry until they are crisp and golden brown (4–5 minutes), then drain on paper towels and serve as soon as all of them are cooked.

Carrot and Spinach Pancakes

Makes 6

¾ cup grated carrots

2 cups chopped fresh leaf
  spinach

1 cup finely chopped onion

2 green chilies, seeded and
  chopped

1 teaspoon aniseed or fennel
  seeds

1 tablespoon ground coriander

½ teaspoon chili powder

1 teaspoon ground turmeric

¾ teaspoon salt, or to taste

1 cup gram flour (besan), sifted

⅓ cup semolina

1 teaspoon baking powder

1¼ cups cold water

oil, for shallow-frying

1) In a large mixing bowl, mix all the ingredients in the list up to and including the salt.

2) In another bowl, mix the gram flour, semolina and baking powder together and add this to the carrot and spinach mixture.

3) Gradually add the water, stirring as you do so with a wooden spoon. Mix until you have a thick batter of spreading consistency.

4) Heat a tablespoon of oil in an iron griddle or a heavy based non-stick skillet over medium heat. Add 2 tablespoons of the pancake mixture and spread it with the back of the spoon until you have a pancake that is about 7 inches in diameter. Cover the pan and cook for 1–2 minutes, or until the pancake is set and the underside has browned a little. Brush the uncooked side with a little oil, then turn the pancake over. Reduce the heat to low and cook for 3–4 minutes or until browned. Repeat with the remainder of the mixture, then serve immediately.

Cook's Note

As you finish each pancake, keep it warm on a baking sheet in an oven set at 225°F while you cook the next one and until you have made all of them. Try to lay them in a single layer as they tend to become soggy if you pile them up.

Pan-Fried Carrot Cake

Makes 10

❧

*B*esides eating this lovely savory "cake" as a snack, you can also serve it as a side dish. I tend to be rather greedy and have two cakes in a hot bun with a bowl of soup and find this makes a complete meal.

1 cup grated carrots
1 small onion, finely chopped
2 green chilies, chopped
½ oz chopped fresh coriander
3 tablespoons all-purpose flour
2 tablespoons semolina

2 large eggs
⅓ cup milk
¾ teaspoon salt, or to taste
¼–½ teaspoon chili powder, optional
oil, for shallow-frying

1) Mix all the ingredients in the list up to and including the semolina together in a mixing bowl.
2) Beat the eggs and milk together in another bowl, then add the salt and chili powder, if using. Beat until well blended and gradually add to the carrot mixture. Mix until all the ingredients are thoroughly mixed together.
3) Heat 2 teaspoons of oil in a small non-stick skillet and put 1 heaped tablespoon of the carrot mixture into the middle of the pan. Spread the mixture out gently with the back of the spoon until you have a 3-inch diameter "cake." If the pan is big enough, slide this cake to one side and make another "cake" in the same way next to it.
4) Cook the "cake" or "cakes" until the underside has browned well, then turn over and cook the other side for 2–3 minutes, or until browned, reducing the heat if it or they start to stick.

Cook's Note

As you finish each "cake" or pair of "cakes," put them on a baking sheet in a low oven while you cook the rest, then serve immediately.

Bread Pakoras
(Bread Fritters)

Serves 4

*H*ere is an idea for livening up stale bread. Pakoras must be eaten hot to enjoy them at their best.

3 tablespoons chili sauce
1 teaspoon mint sauce
1 tablespoon mango chutney,
    mashed to a pulp
6 large slices slightly stale white
    bread, crusts removed
1 cup gram flour (besan)
2 green chilies, chopped
2 tablespoons chopped fresh

coriander
1 teaspoon aniseed
1½ teaspoons garam masala
½ teaspoon ground turmeric
¾ teaspoon salt, or to taste
½ teaspoon chili powder,
    optional
¾ cup cold water
oil, for deep-frying

1) Mix the chili sauce, mint sauce and mango chutney together and use as a spread to make 3 sandwiches with the bread. Cut each sandwich into 4 squares.

2) Mix the remaining ingredients except the water and oil in a bowl and gradually add the cold water, stirring, until you have a thick batter of coating consistency.

3) Heat the oil in a deep pan or wok over medium heat. Test that the temperature is right for frying by dropping a tiny amount of the batter (a drop) into the oil. If it floats quickly to the surface without browning, then the temperature is just right.

4) Dip each sandwich square into the batter. Make sure they are well coated all over, including the edges. Fry them in the hot oil until they are crisp and well browned. Drain on absorbent paper then serve.

Chili and Coriander Toast

Serves 4

❧❦❧

Serve this for breakfast on the weekend—it is sure to wake you up! It is also very good with a bowl of Hearty Vegetable Soup (page 5) as an evening meal.

4 extra large eggs
½ teaspoon salt, or to taste
1 small onion, finely chopped
1–2 fresh green chilies, seeded
    and chopped

2 tablespoons chopped fresh
    coriander leaves
oil and butter, for frying
8 slices of brown or white bread

1) Beat the eggs and add the salt, onion, chilies and coriander. Mix together well.

2) Preheat a small skillet over low heat and add 1 teaspoon oil and ½ teaspoon un-melted butter. When the mixture begins to bubble, fry one side of a slice of bread until it browns, increasing the heat slightly if necessary.

3) With the bread still in the pan, spread 2 tablespoons of the egg mixture on the un-cooked side. Allow the egg to soak into the bread, then turn it over. Let it cook for a minute so the mixture sets, then press it down with a slotted spoon so that the bread sits evenly on the pan. Cook for 1 or 2 minutes, or until it has browned well. Turn it over again and cook the plain side until it is crisp.

Cheese and Coriander Baguettes

Serves 4

*T*his is the perfect accompaniment to any soup.

The quantities given in the recipe are not meant for the full-length baguettes—I used two loaves, which are a little less than half the length of a baguette. You can buy these individually or in a packet from supermarkets.

1 cup grated cheddar, red
    Leicester or flavorful cheese
    of your choice
2 green chilies, seeded and
    chopped

2 tablespoons chopped fresh
    coriander leaves
1 large egg, beaten
2 loaves or 1 medium-sized
    baguette

1) Preheat the broiler to medium.
2) Mix together the cheese, chilies, coriander and egg.
3) Halve the loaves or baguette lengthwise and spread equal quantities of the mixture on each piece of bread.
4) Broil until the topping has browned well, then serve.

Egg Cutlets

Makes 12

❧❀❧

You will need cooked potatoes for this recipe. While you are boiling the eggs, simply cut the potatoes into small pieces and pop them into the microwave or boil them in the usual way. Leave the cooked potatoes in a colander to drain while you continue with the recipe.

Serve the cutlets with Carrot Raita or Coriander and Coconut Chutney (pages 139 and 146).

6 hard-cooked eggs (see above)

2½ cups diced potatoes, boiled (see above) and mashed

3 tablespoons sunflower or soya oil

1 medium onion, finely chopped

1-inch cube gingerroot, peeled and grated

2 green chilies, seeded and chopped

½ teaspoon ground turmeric

½ teaspoon chili powder, or to taste

½ teaspoon garam masala

½ oz chopped fresh coriander

1 teaspoon salt, or to taste

2 tablespoons all-purpose flour

1 extra large egg, beaten

1½ cups fresh soft breadcrumbs

oil, for deep-frying

1) Remove the shells from the eggs and halve them. Scoop out the yolks and mash them. Chop the whites finely and mix the egg yolks and whites with the mashed potatoes.

2) Heat the oil over medium heat and cook the onion, ginger and chilies until the onions have softened, but not browned.

3) Add the spices, coriander and salt. Stir and cook for 1 or 2 minutes, then remove from the heat and add to the potato and egg mixture. Mix until the ingredients are well blended.

4) Heat some oil for deep-frying. Meanwhile, divide the mixture into 12 equal portions and form into oval-shaped cutlets. Coat them lightly with the flour, dip them in the beaten egg, then roll them in the breadcrumbs, making sure they are as evenly coated as possible.

5) Fry the cutlets in the hot oil until they are crisp and have turned golden brown. Drain on absorbent paper then serve immediately.

Spicy Peas with Fried Rolls

Serves 4

A recipe born out of pure necessity. One day I found myself with only a can each of peas and baked beans in my cupboard. I had some lovely, fresh, soft rolls and a couple of bags of potato chips. This may sound like a curious combination, but the end result is quite sensational.

2 tablespoons sunflower or
   soya oil
1 teaspoon cumin seeds
½-inch cube gingerroot, peeled
   and grated
2 garlic cloves, crushed
1 green chili, chopped
½ teaspoon ground turmeric
¼ teaspoon chili powder,
   optional

2 tablespoons chopped fresh
   coriander
½ teaspoon salt, or to taste
14-oz can peas (do not drain)
8-oz can baked beans

To Serve
8 soft rolls and butter
lightly crushed potato chips or
   poppadoms

1) In a saucepan heat the oil over medium heat and throw in the cumin seeds. As soon as they start sizzling, add the ginger, garlic and green chili. Stir-fry until they brown a little.

2) Add the turmeric and chili powder, if using. Stir, then add the coriander, salt, peas and beans. Reduce the heat to low and cook gently until the peas and beans have heated through. Remove from the heat.

3) Split the rolls and butter them to your liking. Now fry them gently, buttered side down first, turning them over once or twice, until the buttered side has browned and is slightly crispy.

4) Top the browned side of the rolls with the pea and bean mixture and sprinkle the crushed chips or poppadoms over the top. Serve immediately.

Cook's Note

If you have any Spicy Peas mixture left over, try it without the rolls. It is simply delicious sprinkled with anything crunchy. If you have some puffed rice cereal, try them—it's lovely!

Spicy Mushroom Omelettes

Makes 2

I love this omelette—with new potatoes diced and cooked in a little butter with a couple of whole garlic cloves, a sprinkling of salt and plenty of freshly ground black pepper ... heavenly! You can also serve it on its own or with oven fries.

2 extra large eggs
¼ cup butter
1 medium onion, finely
   chopped
2 green chilies, seeded and
   chopped

½ teaspoon ground turmeric
2 tablespoons chopped fresh
   coriander
2 cups chopped closed-cap
   mushrooms
½ teaspoon salt, or to taste

1) In a bowl beat the eggs with 2 tablespoons of cold water and set aside.
2) Reserve about 2 teaspoons of butter and melt the remainder over medium heat in an omelette pan or small skillet.
3) Cook the onion and chilies in the butter until the onion is just beginning to brown.
4) Add the turmeric, stir, then add the fresh coriander, mushrooms and salt. Stir them in and fry for 3–4 minutes.
5) Remove half the mushrooms and set them aside.
6) Heat the broiler.
7) Meanwhile, pour half the eggs all around the pan, covering the mushroom mixture completely. Reduce the heat to low and cook until the omelette has set (2–3 min-

utes), then place the pan under the preheated broiler. Cook until the top has set and browned lightly. Fold it in half and serve.

8) Melt the reserved butter in the pan and add the remaining mushroom mixture. Heat through briefly, then pour in the remaining eggs and make a second omelette the same way. Serve.

Onion Bhajias

Makes 18

✦

*H*ere is a lovely recipe for this ever-popular snack. You will find that the home-made version is quite different from that which you may have eaten elsewhere.

1¼ cups gram flour (besan), sifted

⅛ cup ground rice

¼ teaspoon baking soda

1 teaspoon onion seeds (kalonji)

1 teaspoon cumin seeds

1 tablespoon dhanna jeera powder

1 teaspoon ground turmeric

½–1 teaspoon crushed dried chilies

2 green chilies, chopped

1 teaspoon salt, or to taste

½ oz chopped fresh coriander

3 cups halved, sliced onions, divided into rings

¾ cup cold water

oil, for deep-frying

1) In a large mixing bowl, mix together the gram flour, ground rice and soda. Add the remaining ingredients except the fresh coriander, onions, cold water and oil. Mix thoroughly.

2) Add the coriander and onions and gradually pour in the cold water. Mix until the gram flour and spices coat the onions. The batter should lightly bind the onions so that you can pick up small portions with your fingers. Indeed, you will find that using your fingers to make bhajias will work better than anything else.

3) Heat the oil in a deep-fryer or wok over a medium heat. Check that the temperature is correct by pouring a drop of the batter into the hot oil. If it floats immediately to the surface without browning, then the oil is at just the right temperature.

4) When the oil is ready, pick up a small portion of the onion mixture—it needs to be roughly the size of a golf ball—and flatten it slightly so that it is not too compact. Repeat and fry them in batches (they should be in a single layer) in the hot oil for 8–9 minutes, or until they have browned all over. Make sure that the temperature of the oil stays about the same throughout. Drain each batch on paper towels and serve once you have cooked all of the mixture.

Paneer Tikkis (Cheese Patties)

Makes 8

Serve with a salad or make vegetarian hamburgers by putting them into hot split rolls together with a relish such as Carrot, Sweet Corn or Mushroom Raita (pages 139, 138 or 140) or tomato ketchup.

2 large slices slightly stale white bread

1 cup water

1 cup roughly chopped paneer or Cyprus halloumi cheese

15–20 chopped fresh mint leaves or ½ teaspoon dried mint

2 tablespoons chopped fresh coriander

½-inch cube gingerroot, peeled and grated

¼ cup slivered almonds, lightly crushed

1–2 green chilies, chopped

1 teaspoon garam masala

½ teaspoon chili powder, optional

1 teaspoon salt, or to taste

1 tablespoon lemon juice

1 large egg, beaten

oil, for shallow-frying

1) Soak the slices of bread in the water for 1 or 2 minutes, then squeeze out all the water by pressing them between your palms.

2) Place the pieces of soaked bread in a large mixing bowl and add the remaining ingredients, except the oil. Mix well until the ingredients bind together.

3) Divide the mixture in half and make 4 equal-sized flat cakes ¼-inch thick.

4) Pour oil into a frying pan until it is 1 inch deep and heat over medium heat. Fry the Tikkis until they have browned well on both sides. Drain on paper towels.

Savory Semolina

Serves 4

Semolina is used in a variety of recipes in India, both savory and sweet. Here is a popular savory breakfast recipe from southern India. It is delicious and filling.

2 tablespoons shredded
coconut

2¾ cups hot water

1 cup semolina

4 tablespoons sunflower or
soya oil

1 teaspoon black mustard seeds

1 teaspoon cumin seeds

1 long, slim, dried red chili,
chopped

12–15 fresh curry leaves

1 large onion, finely chopped
(minced)

1–2 green chilies, chopped
(seeded, too, if you wish)

1 teaspoon garam masala

2 tablespoons seedless raisins

2 tablespoons broken cashew
pieces

½ cup frozen peas

1 teaspoon salt, or to taste

1 tablespoon lemon juice

2 tablespoons chopped fresh
coriander

1) Put the coconut in a bowl and pour ⅓ cup of the hot water over it. Set aside.

2) Heat a heavy pan over medium heat and dry roast the semolina for 10 minutes, or until it is golden brown. Stir it constantly to ensure that it browns evenly. Remove the pan from the heat and set aside.

3) Heat the oil over medium heat until it is quite hot, but not smoking. Throw in the mustard seeds, then the cumin, red chili and curry leaves.

4) Add the onion and green chilies. Stir-fry them until the onion has softened, but not browned.

5) Add the garam masala, raisins and cashews. Fry for 1–2 minutes, then pour in the rest of the hot water.

6) Add the peas, salt, soaked coconut with its water, lemon juice, fresh coriander and roasted semolina. Stir and cook for 5–6 minutes over low heat, or until the semolina has absorbed all the water, then serve.

Semolina Pancakes

Makes 12

*D*elicious savory pancakes which are very nutritious and sustaining.

1¼ cups semolina

1 teaspoon salt, or to taste

½ teaspoon baking soda

1 medium onion, finely
   chopped

1 teaspoon finely grated gingerroot

2 green chilies, seeded and
   chopped

1 teaspoon cumin seeds

2 tablespoons chopped fresh
   coriander

¾ cup plain yogurt

1¼ cups cold water

sunflower or soya oil, for
   shallow-frying

1) In a large mixing bowl, mix the semolina with the salt and baking soda. Add the remaining ingredients except the yogurt, water and oil, stirring and mixing them together thoroughly.

2) Blend the yogurt with the water and gradually add this to the semolina mixture.
   Mix them together until a thick paste is formed.

3) Spread 2 teaspoons of oil in an iron griddle or a small, non-stick, heavy skillet and
   heat over medium-low heat. Put 1 heaped tablespoon of the semolina paste into the
   center of the pan and gently spread it with the back of the spoon to form a
   3-inch diameter pancake. Cover the pan with a lid and let the pancake cook for
   about 2 minutes.

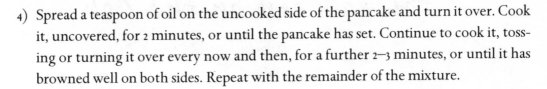

4) Spread a teaspoon of oil on the uncooked side of the pancake and turn it over. Cook it, uncovered, for 2 minutes, or until the pancake has set. Continue to cook it, tossing or turning it over every now and then, for a further 2–3 minutes, or until it has browned well on both sides. Repeat with the remainder of the mixture.

Cook's Note

As you finish each pancake, put it on a baking sheet in the oven, set at 225°F, to keep warm until you have finished cooking all of them. Place them in a single layer so they stay nice and crisp.

Spiced Corn on the Cob

Serves 4

*I*n India, we use fresh corn cobs, but you can use frozen ones, too. As they need slicing, thawing them slightly in the microwave will make it easier.

Serve with anything from a bowl of lentils or soup to Chili and Coriander Toast (page 21) and your favorite cocktail.

¼ cup shredded coconut

2–4 dried red chilies, chopped

⅔ cup hot water

4 corn on the cob, fresh or frozen

1 teaspoon salt, or to taste

1 tablespoon sunflower or soya oil

½ teaspoon black mustard seeds

½ teaspoon cumin seeds

2–3 green chilies, seeded and chopped

1 tablespoon chopped fresh coriander

1½ tablespoons lemon juice

1) Put the coconut and red chilies in a bowl and pour the hot water over them. Cover and set aside for 5 minutes.

2) Meanwhile, slice the corn cobs into ½-inch thick rounds.

3) Put the coconut and chilies into a blender and blend until smooth. Put into a roomy saucepan with the corn and add the salt. Heat gently until it is just simmering, cover and cook for 10 minutes, stirring halfway through.

4) Meanwhile, heat the oil in a small saucepan over medium heat. When it is hot, but not smoking, add the mustard seeds, followed by the cumin. Let them pop for 5–10 seconds then pour the contents over the corn.

5) Add the green chilies, fresh coriander and lemon juice. Stir until all the liquid evaporates and you only have the coconut and spices left, coating the corn. Remove from the heat and serve.

Stuffed Croissants

Serves 4

These are wonderful for a weekend brunch or a light lunch. They taste good hot or cold, so they are great for picnics.

2 tablespoons sunflower or soya oil	2 tablespoons chopped fresh coriander
2 tablespoons butter	½ teaspoon ground turmeric
1 medium onion, finely chopped	½ teaspoon salt, or to taste
1–2 green chilies, seeded and chopped	4 eggs
	4 croissants

1) Heat the oil and butter together in an omelette pan or small skillet and cook the onion and chilies until the onion has softened.

2) Add the fresh coriander, turmeric and salt. Cook for 1 minute and remove the mixture from the pan, then divide it into quarters.

3) Return one portion of the onion mixture to the pan and add a little more oil or butter if necessary. Then, beat 1 of the eggs with 2 tablespoons of water and pour it all over the onion mixture. Cook until the omelette has set and the underside has browned. If you like both sides to be brown, you can quickly brown the top under the broiler. Fold the omelette in half and remove it from the pan. Make 3 more omelettes the same way.

4) Warm the croissants briefly under the broiler or in the microwave and split them. Cut the omelettes into thick strips, fill the croissants with them and serve.

Mushroom-Topped Crumpets

Serves 4

*E*at these as a snack or make a complete meal by having them with a bowl of soup.

¼ cup butter
1 small onion, finely chopped
1–2 green chilies, chopped
1 teaspoon ground cumin
1 cup chopped fresh tomatoes
2 tablespoons chopped fresh
   coriander

2 cups chopped closed-cap
   mushrooms
salt, to taste
8 crumpets
¾ cup grated cheddar or other
   flavorful cheese

1) In a skillet melt the butter over medium heat and cook the onion and green chilies until the onion has softened.
2) Add the cumin, tomatoes and fresh coriander. Stir, then add the mushrooms and season with salt to taste. Mix thoroughly and remove from the heat.
3) Place crumpets upside down on a broiler pan and broil for 1 or 2 minutes.
4) Remove the pan from the broiler and turn the crumpets over. Divide the mushroom mixture equally between the crumpets and top with the grated cheese. Broil until the cheese is bubbling and turning golden brown.

Vegetarian Burgers

Makes 8

These burgers, made with soya mince, are delicious and filling. Serve them with Spicy French Fries and Tomato and Cucumber Raita (pages 103 and 145). Alternatively, serve them with ketchup and crisp lettuce leaves in soft buns.

1 cup soya mince

1 small onion, finely chopped

1–2 fresh green chilies, seeded and chopped

1 cup hot water

1 teaspoon ground coriander

1 teaspoon ground cumin

1 teaspoon garam masala

2 tablespoons chopped fresh coriander leaves

1 tablespoon tomato paste

1 teaspoon salt, or to taste

1 oz ground rice

2 extra large eggs, beaten

oil, for shallow-frying

1 oz all-purpose flour

1) Put the soya mince into a large mixing bowl with the onion and chilies and pour in the hot water. Mix everything together thoroughly, then add the remaining ingredients except the oil and flour.

2) While the mixture is still hot (it is difficult to shape the burgers when the mixture is cold, so make sure you do this while it is hot), divide it in half and make 4 equal-sized balls out of each half. Flatten the balls to form burger shapes, then set them aside for 10 minutes. If the mixture sticks to your fingers, lightly grease the palms of your hands and fingers.

3) Pour enough oil into a skillet to cover the base of it to a depth of about ½ inch and heat over medium heat. Dust burgers with some of the flour, then fry them gently in the oil for 3–4 minutes on each side, until they have browned well. Drain on absorbent paper then serve.

Main Meals

The recipes in this chapter are based on an exciting variety of ingredients that are high in protein. This, combined with the fact that they are easy to prepare and quick to make, means that you cannot fail to be delighted by the sensational results.

When you are choosing a menu, pay particular attention to the length of simmering or slow cooking time specified in each recipe. It is vital to utilize these times when you do not have to attend to a dish to prepare or even, perhaps, cook another dish. There are plenty of very quick recipes in the Side Dishes chapter that you can easily make while the main dish is cooking. Remember, you don't want to be in the kitchen too long, but feeling totally satisfied when you've finished your meal is important, too!

Broccoli with Eggs

Serves 4

A simple, nutritious and visually appealing dish that only takes about 10 minutes to cook. Serve it with warmed chapattis, Cumin and Coriander Bread (page 136) or any other plain or flavored bread you like.

3 tablespoons sunflower or
  soya oil
1 large red onion, finely sliced
2 green chilies, seeded and
  sliced
½ teaspoon ground turmeric
1 teaspoon ground cumin

3½ cups small broccoli florets
1 teaspoon salt, or to taste
4 extra large eggs, beaten

1) In a skillet heat the oil over medium heat and cook the onion and chilies for 3–4 minutes, stirring frequently.

2) Add the turmeric and cumin and cook for 30 seconds.

3) Add the broccoli and salt, increase the heat to high and stir-fry the broccoli for 2–3 minutes, or until the broccoli starts to color. Then, reduce the heat to low, cover the pan and cook for 5 more minutes.

4) Pour the beaten eggs all around the pan and over the broccoli. Stir for a few minutes until you have softly scrambled eggs coating the broccoli, then remove from the heat and serve.

Eggplant, Egg and Potato Curry

Serves 4

*T*he eggplant, gently simmered in coconut milk and spices, becomes soft, velvety and inviting. You can use more than one egg per person if you wish and serve with warmed naan or pita.

4 hard-cooked eggs

4 tablespoons sunflower or
  soya oil

1 large onion, finely chopped

1-inch cube gingerroot, peeled
  and grated

4 large garlic cloves, crushed
  (minced)

1 teaspoon ground cumin

2 teaspoons ground coriander

½ teaspoon ground turmeric

½ teaspoon chili powder

1 teaspoon garam masala

1½ cups cubed potatoes (1-inch
  cubes)

1 teaspoon salt, or to taste

½ cup coconut milk powder

2 cups hot water

2 cups cubed eggplant (1-inch
  cubes)

¼ cup creamed coconut, grated

½ cup chopped fresh tomatoes

4 whole green chilies

2 tablespoons chopped fresh
  coriander

1) Remove the shells from the eggs and make 6 slits lengthwise on each egg. Set them aside.

2) In a skillet heat the oil over medium heat and cook the onion, ginger and garlic for 5–6 minutes, until the onions have softened but not browned.

3) In a small bowl mix the cumin, coriander, turmeric, chili powder and garam masala, add enough water to make a paste of pouring consistency and add it to the onion mixture. Cook for 2–3 minutes, stirring frequently, and add 2 tablespoons water. Continue to cook for 2 minutes.

4) Add the potatoes, salt and coconut milk powder blended with the hot water. Bring to a slow simmer, cover and cook for 5–6 minutes.

5) Add the eggplant, creamed coconut and eggs. Stir once, cover the pan once more and simmer gently for a further 5–6 minutes.

6) Add the tomatoes, fresh chilies and coriander. Simmer, uncovered, for 2–3 minutes, then remove from the heat and serve.

Lima Beans with Carrots and Green Beans

Serves 4

Serve with Tomato and Coriander Rice or Tarka Rice (pages 127 and 132).

1½ cups very thickly sliced carrots (1½-inch thick slices)

2 cups green beans (1-inch pieces)

2 cups hot water

1 tablespoon coriander seeds

2–3 long, slim, dried red chilies, chopped

⅓ cup shredded coconut, grated

⅓ cup creamed coconut, grated

1½ cups canned, drained lima beans

1 teaspoon salt, or to taste

1 tablespoon ghee or unsalted butter

4–5 large garlic cloves, minced

½ teaspoon ground turmeric

1) Put the carrots and green beans in a saucepan and add the hot water. Bring to a boil, then reduce the heat, cover the pan and simmer gently for 6–7 minutes.

2) Meanwhile, preheat a small, heavy skillet and dry roast the coriander seeds and chilies for a minute or so. Then, remove the pan from the heat and allow to cool.

3) When the coriander and chilies have cooled, grind them in a coffee grinder for a couple of seconds, then add the shredded coconut and grind for a few seconds until you have a fine powdery mixture. Add this to the vegetables.

4) Add the creamed coconut, lima beans and salt. Cover and simmer for 4–5 minutes.

5) Heat the ghee or butter in a small saucepan and cook the garlic until it has browned. Add the turmeric and cook for 10–15 seconds, then stir this into the carrot, bean and lima bean mixture. Remove from the heat and serve.

Chickpeas (Garbanzos) in Coconut Milk

Serves 4

*I*have used canned chickpeas (garbanzos) here because the aim in this book is to be time-efficient, but if you want to use dried chickpeas (garbanzos), they are easy to cook. Simply soak them overnight and boil them in fresh water for 10 minutes and then simmer, covered, until they are tender (about 1½ hours, although they can vary quite a lot in the time they take, so check them after an hour and every 15 minutes or so after that). You will need to cook about ¾ cup dried chickpeas (garbanzos) to make this recipe.

Serve this dish with either boiled basmati rice or Tarka Rice and a raita (pages 132 and 138–145).

½ cup coconut milk powder
2 cups hot water
2 cups peeled and cubed
  potatoes (1-inch cubes)
14-oz can chickpeas
  (garbanzos), drained and
  well rinsed
5–6 garlic cloves, peeled and
  roughly chopped

1 teaspoon salt, or to taste
2 tablespoons sunflower or
  soya oil
1½ teaspoons ground coriander
½ teaspoon ground turmeric
½ teaspoon chili powder
level ½ teaspoon tamarind
  juice or 1½ tablespoons lime
  juice

1) Blend the coconut milk powder with the hot water in a saucepan and add the pota-toes. Cover the pan, bring to a boil, then reduce the heat to low and cook for 6–7 minutes.

2) Add the chickpeas (garbanzos), cover and cook for 3–4 minutes, or until the pota-toes are tender.

3) Meanwhile, mince the garlic and salt together until you have a smooth pulp. This is easy to do in a mortar with a pestle, but if you do not have these, the back of a wooden spoon or the blade of a large knife does the job just as well.

4) Heat the oil in a small saucepan over medium heat and cook the garlic and salt mix-ture until it starts to brown. Then, add the coriander, turmeric and chili powder and stir-fry for 30 seconds.

5) Add this mixture to the potato and chickpea (garbanzo) mixture, scraping every lit-tle bit of the spice mixture out of the pan.

6) Add the tamarind or lime juice, stirring and mixing it in well, then simmer for 2–3 minutes, uncovered, before removing the pan from the heat and serving.

Chickpeas (Garbanzos) with Vegetables

Serves 4

A quick, easy and completely balanced dish with an enticing flavor. Simply serve it with any bread or Cumin Rice (page 122).

1½ cups peeled and cubed
  potatoes (1-inch cubes)
1½ cups cut green beans (1-inch
  pieces)
3¼ cups hot water
½ cup coconut milk powder
1¼ cups drained and rinsed
  canned chickpeas
  (garbanzos)

½ cup creamed coconut, grated
1 teaspoon salt, or to taste
1 tablespoon sunflower or soya
  oil
1 tablespoon ground coriander
½ teaspoon ground turmeric
½–1 teaspoon chili powder
1½ tablespoons lime juice

1) Put the potatoes and beans into a saucepan together with 2 cups of the hot water and bring to a boil over high heat. Then cover the pan, reduce the heat to medium and cook for 5 minutes.

2) Blend the coconut milk powder with the remainder of the hot water and add this mixture and the chickpeas (garbanzos) to the pan and let the mixture return to a gentle simmer before stirring in the creamed coconut and salt. Cover the pan and simmer gently for 6–8 minutes.

3) Meanwhile, heat the oil in a small saucepan over low heat. Add the coriander, turmeric and chili powder and cook gently for 30 seconds.

4) Stir the cooked spices into the potato, bean and chickpea (garbanzo) mixture, then add the lime juice. Remove the pan from the heat and keep it tightly covered until you are ready to serve to lock in the flavors.

Egg and Potato Curry

Serves 4

*S*erve this tasty curry with Cumin Rice (page 122).

4 hard-cooked eggs

4 tablespoons sunflower or
   soya oil

1 large onion, finely chopped

two 1-inch pieces cassia bark or
   cinnamon stick

3 large garlic cloves, minced

½-inch cube gingerroot, peeled
   and grated

½ teaspoon ground cumin

1 teaspoon ground coriander

½ teaspoon ground turmeric

½ teaspoon chili powder

1 tablespoon ground almonds

2½ cups medium-sized
   potatoes, quartered

1 teaspoon salt, or to taste

1¼ cups hot water

2 tablespoons light cream

⅔ cup sour cream

½ teaspoon garam masala

2 tablespoons chopped fresh
   coriander leaves

4 whole green chilies

1–2 chunkily chopped fresh
   tomatoes, to garnish,
   optional

1) Remove the shells from the eggs and make 5–6 deep slits lengthwise in each of them. This allows the flavors to penetrate the eggs. Set them aside.

2) In a saucepan heat the oil over medium heat and cook the onion, cassia bark or cinnamon stick, garlic and ginger for 5–6 minutes, until the onion has softened, but not browned.

3) In a small bowl, mix together the cumin, coriander, turmeric and chili powder and add enough water to make a mixture of pouring consistency. Add this to the onion, stir it in, then cook for 2–3 minutes.

4) Add the ground almonds and cook for 1 minute.

5) Add the potatoes, salt and hot water. Bring to a boil, then reduce the heat, cover and simmer gently for 10 minutes.

6) Add the eggs, both types of cream, garam masala, coriander leaves and chilies. Cover and simmer for 8–10 minutes more, or until the potatoes are tender.

7) Remove from the heat, transfer to a warmed serving dish, garnish with the chopped tomatoes, if using, and serve.

Eggs with Lentils

Serves 4

*T*he combination of eggs with lentils makes for a substantial and very tasty dish. Serve it with any bread you like or boiled basmati rice. A raita is nice with this, too, if you have time to make one (pages 138–145).

4 hard-cooked eggs
1 cup dried red split lentils
  (masoor dhal)
4 tablespoons ghee or unsalted
  butter
1 teaspoon ground turmeric
2 bay leaves, crumbled
two 1-inch pieces of cassia bark
  or cinnamon stick
1 large onion, finely chopped
½-inch cube gingerroot, peeled
  and grated
2 long, slim, dried red chilies,
  chopped

1 tablespoon ground coriander
1 teaspoon ground cumin
1¾ cups skinned, chopped
  tomatoes or canned tomatoes with juice
¾ cup hot water
1 teaspoon salt, or to taste
1–2 green chilies, seeded and
  sliced
2 tablespoons chopped fresh
  coriander

1) Remove the shells from the eggs and make at least 6 slits lengthwise in each egg so that the flavors can penetrate them. Set them aside.
2) Wash the lentils at least twice in cold water and leave them to drain in a colander.

3) In a skillet heat the ghee or butter over a medium heat and add half the turmeric and all the eggs. Cook them, rolling them around in the pan until they have browned all over and this forms a light crust. Then, remove the eggs with a slotted spoon and set them aside.

4) In the same pan, cook the bay leaves and pieces of cassia bark or cinnamon stick for 15–20 seconds.

5) Add the onion, ginger and red chilies. Stir and cook for 6–7 minutes, until the onions have browned lightly.

6) Add the lentils, the remaining turmeric, ground coriander and cumin and stir-fry for 5–6 minutes.

7) Add half the tomatoes and cook, stirring frequently, for 3–4 minutes.

8) Pour the hot water into the pan, bring to a boil, then reduce the heat, cover the pan and simmer gently for 20 minutes.

9) Add the salt, the remaining tomatoes and the eggs. Cover and simmer for 7–8 more minutes.

10) Add the green chilies and fresh coriander, simmer for 2–3 minutes, then remove from the heat and serve.

South Indian Fried Eggs

Serves 4

*T*his is based on a recipe known as Egg Roast, which I first came across in Kerala, southern India. The "roast" turned out to be hard-cooked eggs that were fried with spices until they had browned—seriously delicious! I have added potatoes here in my version of this dish to make a more substantial meal.

This dish is good served with warmed chapattis or any dhal you like and boiled basmati rice.

4 hard-cooked eggs
5 tablespoons sunflower or
   soya oil
1 teaspoon cumin seeds
3¼ cups very thickly sliced
   potatoes (1-inch thick slices)
½ teaspoon chili powder
½ teaspoon ground turmeric
½ teaspoon salt, or to taste
½ teaspoon freshly ground
   black pepper

½-inch cube gingerroot, peeled
   and grated
2 garlic cloves, minced
1 large onion, finely sliced
1 cup chopped fresh tomatoes
1–2 green chilies, seeded and
   chopped
2 tablespoons chopped fresh
   coriander leaves

1) Remove the shells from the eggs and make at least 6 deep slits lengthwise on each of them to enable them to absorb the flavors. Set them aside.

2) Heat 2 tablespoons of the oil in a large, non-stick skillet over medium heat and add the cumin seeds. Let them sizzle for 15–20 seconds.

3) Add the potatoes, half the chili powder and half the turmeric and salt. Stir, cover the pan and cook for 5–10 minutes, stirring occasionally, or until the potatoes are tender and brown.

4) Stir in the black pepper, transfer the mixture to a heatproof dish and keep warm while you continue to cook the rest of the dish.

5) Add 2 tablespoons of the oil to the skillet and cook the ginger and garlic for 1 minute.

6) Add the onion and stir-fry for 8–9 minutes, or until it has caramelized and turned golden brown. Reduce heat slightly towards the end if necessary.

7) Add salt to taste and spread the onion on top of the potatoes. Keep hot.

8) Heat the remainder of the oil in the same pan over medium heat. When it is hot, remove the pan from the heat and add the remaining chili powder and turmeric and the eggs. Return the pan to the heat and cook the eggs, stirring constantly, until they have browned evenly.

9) Add the tomatoes, chilies and coriander leaves. Stir and cook gently for 2–3 minutes.

10) Season to taste, arrange the eggs on the potato and onion mixture and serve.

Spicy Green Lentils

Serves 4

These lentils are flat and green and readily available. Though they are not grown in India, they are excellent to cook with spices. They are particularly good served with Coconut or Lemon Rice (pages 123 and 126), and Paneer Bhujia (page 77) makes an excellent accompaniment.

1 cup green lentils	1–2 green chilies, chopped
3¾ cups hot water	1–2 dried red chilies, chopped
3 tablespoons sunflower or	½ teaspoon ground turmeric
soya oil	½ cup chopped fresh tomatoes
1 teaspoon cumin seeds	1 teaspoon salt, or to taste
2 bay leaves, crumbled	2 tablespoons chopped fresh
1 medium onion, chopped	coriander
3–4 large garlic cloves, minced	

1) Wash the lentils and put them into a saucepan with the hot water. Bring to a boil, then cover, reduce the heat and simmer for 20–25 minutes.

2) Meanwhile, in a skillet heat the oil over medium heat and add the cumin seeds and bay leaves. Let them sizzle gently for 15–20 seconds.

3) Add the onion, garlic and both types of chilies. Cook them for 6–7 minutes, until the onion has caramelized and turned golden brown.

4) Add the turmeric and tomatoes. Cook for a minute or so and, when the lentils are ready, stir this spicy mixture and the salt into the lentils. Bring to a boil, add the fresh coriander, then remove from the heat and serve.

Hot and Spicy Quorn

Serves 4

Quorn is a natural food that is extremely tasty as well as full of protein, high in fiber and low in fat. When it is cooked with exotic spices and served with Lemon Rice (page 126) or naan or pita bread and a raita (pages 138–145), it is irresistible!

3 tablespoons sunflower or
  soya oil

1 large onion, finely chopped

3–4 garlic cloves, minced

1-inch cube gingerroot, peeled
  and grated

1–2 green chilies, chopped
  (seeded if wished)

12-oz packet minced Quorn
  (available at natural food
  shops)

1 teaspoon ground turmeric

1½ teaspoons ground coriander

1 teaspoon ground cumin

1 cup canned chopped
  tomatoes with juice

1 cup hot water

1 teaspoon salt, or to taste

1 cup frozen peas

½ teaspoon garam masala

1 tablespoon chopped fresh or
  1 teaspoon dried mint

2 tablespoons chopped fresh
  coriander

3 tablespoons light cream

1) In a skillet heat the oil over medium heat and cook the onion, garlic, ginger and green chilies until the onion has softened, but not browned.

2) Add the Quorn and stir-fry for 3–4 minutes.

3) Add the spices and tomatoes, stir and cook for 2–3 minutes.

4) Pour in the hot water and add the salt. Stir and bring to a boil, then reduce the heat and simmer, covered, for 15 minutes.

5) Add the remaining ingredients, stir, increase the heat slightly and cook gently for 3–4 minutes.

6) Remove from the heat and serve.

Lentils with Green Beans

Serves 4

Adelicious combination that also provides you with protein and vitamins. Have it with Cumin or Hot Mushroom Rice (pages 122 and 125) or some warmed naan or pita bread.

1 cup dried split yellow lentils (moong dhal)

1½ cups cut green beans (1-inch pieces)

1 teaspoon ground turmeric

3½ cups hot water

2 teaspoons sunflower or soya oil

2–4 long, slim, dried red chilies, chopped

¾ teaspoon fenugreek seeds

½ cup coconut milk powder

1 teaspoon salt, or to taste

1½ tablespoons lime juice

1) Wash and drain the lentils and put them into a saucepan with the beans, turmeric and 2½ cups of the hot water. Place over high heat, bring to a boil and boil for 2–3 minutes, then reduce the heat and cook, uncovered, for 10 minutes.

2) Meanwhile, heat the oil in a small saucepan over low heat and cook the chilies and fenugreek seeds until they have turned a shade darker. Then, remove the pan from the heat and leave them to cool.

3) When the chilies and fenugreek seeds are cool enough to handle, crush them with the oil until you have a paste. You can do this in the pan itself, using a wooden pestle or the back of a wooden spoon.

4) Blend the coconut milk powder with the remainder of the hot water and add to the lentils and beans together with the salt. Heat until it is gently simmering and then leave it to cook, uncovered, for 5 minutes.

5) Add the chili and fenugreek paste and lime juice. Stir once, then simmer for 2–3 minutes.

6) Remove from the heat and serve.

Lentils with Zucchini

Serves 4

*T*omato and Coriander or Coconut Rice (pages 127 and 123) are very good with this; otherwise, any bread you happen to have, plain or flavored, would go with it very well.

1 cup dried split yellow lentils
(moong dhal)

¼ cup ghee or unsalted butter

6 green cardamom pods

1 teaspoon royal cumin (shahi
jeera)

6 whole cloves

1 large onion, finely sliced

4 large garlic cloves, minced

1-inch cube gingerroot, peeled
and grated

½ teaspoon crushed dried
chilies

1 teaspoon ground turmeric

2 teaspoons ground cumin

2½ cups hot water

1 teaspoon salt, or to taste

2 cups bite-sized pieces of
zucchini

½ teaspoon garam masala

2 tablespoons chopped fresh
coriander leaves

1) Wash the lentils thoroughly and leave to drain in a colander.
2) In a saucepan heat the ghee or butter over medium heat.
3) Meanwhile, peel back each cardamom pod very slightly and add to the fat along with the royal cumin and cloves. Let them sizzle for 15–20 seconds.
4) Add the onion, garlic, ginger and chilies. Stir-fry for 7–8 minutes, until the onion has caramelized and turned golden brown.

5) Add the lentils, turmeric and ground cumin and stir-fry for 2 minutes before pouring in the hot water.

6) Bring to a boil, reduce the heat, cover the pan and simmer gently for 15–20 minutes. Stir once or twice during cooking to prevent the mixture from sticking.

7) Add the salt, zucchini and garam masala, stir, cover once more and continue to simmer for another 2–3 minutes.

8) Stir in the coriander leaves, remove from the heat and serve.

Mixed Dhal with Spiced Butter (Mixed Lentils with Spiced Butter)

Serves 4

The combination of whole spices used to season this dhal consists of five types of seeds you will find in your pantry. If possible, season the dhal about ten minutes before you are going to eat and keep the saucepan tightly covered. Then, when you remove the lid at the table, the aroma will bring your taste buds to life!

Ideal accompaniments to this dish are boiled basmati rice and a dry, spiced dish, such as Paneer with Peppers, Cauliflower with Sesame Seeds (pages 73 and 92), or a raita (pages 138–145).

½ cup dried split red lentils (masoor dhal)

½ cup dried split yellow lentils (moong dhal)

3¾ cups hot water

1 teaspoon salt, or to taste

1 tablespoon lemon juice

2 tablespoons chopped fresh coriander

2 tablespoons ghee or clarified butter (see Note)

¼ teaspoon black mustard seeds

¼ teaspoon cumin seeds

¼ teaspoon onion seeds

¼ teaspoon fennel seeds

8–10 fenugreek seeds

14–16 fresh curry leaves

4 small dried red chilies

½ teaspoon ground turmeric

1) Mix both types of lentils together, wash them thoroughly, then drain. Put them into a saucepan with the hot water, bring to a boil, then reduce the heat slightly and leave them to boil for 5–6 minutes.

2) Reduce the heat further, cover and simmer the lentils gently for 20 minutes.

3) Add the salt and lemon juice to the pan and beat the lentils with a wire whisk. Add a little more hot water if the mixture is too thick.

4) Add the fresh coriander and leave the saucepan over very low heat while you prepare the spiced butter.

5) Heat the ghee over medium heat. When it is quite hot, but not smoking, add the mustard seeds. As soon as they begin to pop, reduce the heat to low and add the remaining ingredients, except the turmeric. Let the spices sizzle until the seeds begin to pop and the chilies have blackened.

6) Stir in the turmeric and pour the spices and the butter over the lentil mixture, scraping every last bit from the saucepan.

7) Turn off the heat and keep the saucepan covered until you are ready to eat.

Cook's Note

To make clarified butter, use unsalted butter cut into 1-inch pieces. In a heavy saucepan melt the butter over low heat for 20–30 minutes, or until the butter stops crackling. Remove from heat and let stand about 3 minutes and skim the froth. Strain the butter through a lined sieve. Pour the clarified butter into a jar and store it, covered, in an air-tight container, at room temperature. The butter keeps up to 8 months.

Moong Dhal with Spinach (Dried Split Yellow Lentils with Spinach)

Serves 4

With lentils and spinach in one dish, you need only bread or rice to accompany it, and Coconut or Hot Mushroom Rice are ideal (pages 123 and 125).

1 cup dried split yellow lentils (moong dhal)

2½ cups hot water

3 cups chopped spinach, fresh or frozen

1 teaspoon salt, or to taste

3 tablespoons sunflower or soya oil

1 large onion, finely sliced

1-inch cube gingerroot, peeled and grated

1–2 green chilies, chopped

12–14 fresh curry leaves

1 teaspoon ground turmeric

½ cup chopped fresh tomatoes

1) Rinse the lentils really well and drain, then put them into a saucepan with the hot water and bring to a boil. Then, reduce the heat a little and simmer, uncovered, for 10 minutes.

2) Add the spinach and salt. Cook until the spinach has wilted (in the case of frozen spinach, until it has thawed).

3) Reduce the heat further, cover the pan and simmer gently for 8–10 minutes, or until the lentils and spinach are tender.

4) Meanwhile, in a large skillet heat the oil over medium heat and cook the onion, ginger, chilies and curry leaves for 6–7 minutes stirring frequently, until the onions have caramelized and turned golden brown.

5) Add the turmeric to the onion mixture and stir it in, then add this to the lentil and spinach mixture. Add the tomatoes and cook for 2–3 minutes.

6) Remove from the heat and serve.

Tarka Dhal
(Seasoned Lentils)

Serves 4

'*T*arka' means seasoning. There are various recipes for the seasoning for a Tarka Dhal, which can vary quite a lot, but this is one of the simplest. Serve with Baby Vegetable Pulao or Tomato and Coriander Rice (pages 118 and 127) and a raita (pages 138–145).

1½ cups dried split yellow lentils (moong dhal)

2½ cups hot water

1 teaspoon salt, or to taste

2 tablespoons ghee

½ teaspoon black mustard seeds

2 large garlic cloves, minced

½–1 teaspoon crushed dried chilies

1 teaspoon ground turmeric

1 teaspoon garam masala

2 tablespoons chopped fresh coriander leaves

1 tablespoon lemon juice

1) Wash and drain the lentils before putting them into a saucepan with the hot water. Bring to a boil over high heat and let it boil for 5 minutes. Then, reduce the heat, cover the pan and simmer gently for 10–12 minutes. Stir in the salt when this time has passed.

2) In a skillet heat the ghee (butter is not suitable as this dish needs to be cooked at a high temperature) over medium heat until it is quite hot, but not smoking. Add the mustard seeds and, as soon as they pop, add the garlic and allow the garlic to brown slightly.

3) Add the chilies, turmeric, and garam masala, stir for 10–15 seconds, then pour the mixture into the lentils.

4) Stir in the coriander leaves and lemon juice. Remove the pan from the heat and keep the saucepan tightly covered until you are ready to serve to keep the flavors locked in.

Nepalese Dhal (Nepalese Lentils)

Serves 4

Lentils are a favorite of mine. A hot crusty roll and a bowlful of dhal enlivened with spices is a meal we often enjoy at home. Alternatively, try this with Cumin Rice (page 122) and a raita (pages 138–145).

1 cup dried split red lentils (masoor dhal)

¼ cup ghee or unsalted butter

1 large onion, finely chopped

1–2 fresh green chilies, seeded and chopped

1 teaspoon ground turmeric

2 teaspoons ground coriander

2 teaspoons ground cumin

1½ teaspoons garam masala

1¼ teaspoons salt, or to taste

3¾ cups hot water

2 tablespoons chopped fresh coriander leaves

1) Wash and rinse the lentils 2–3 times, then set them aside to drain in a colander.

2) Heat the ghee or butter gently in a non-stick saucepan over low heat and add the onion and chilies. Increase the heat a little and cook for 6–8 minutes, until the onion has browned lightly.

3) Add the spices, stir-fry them for 30 seconds, then add the lentils and salt. Cook for 3–4 minutes, until the lentils are dry and look quite separate from each other.

4) Pour in the hot water and bring to a boil. Then, reduce the heat, cover the pan and simmer very gently for 25 minutes.

5) Stir in the coriander leaves, remove from the heat and serve.

Paneer with Peppers (Cheese with Peppers)

Serves 4

As this recipe takes just ten minutes to make, you will have ample time to cook whatever else you fancy. It is particularly good served with a dhal of your choice (pages 66–72) and plain rice or a raita (pages 138–145) and Cumin and Coriander Bread (page 136).

Note that you will need to use half the quantity of salt given in the recipe if you use halloumi cheese as it is salty, unlike paneer.

1½ teaspoons cumin seeds	½ teaspoon chili powder
2 tablespoons sunflower or soya oil	1 teaspoon salt, or to taste (see above)
2 cups sliced onions	1 cup thickly sliced paneer or Cyprus halloumi cheese
2 cups roughly chopped green bell peppers	
2 cups roughly chopped red bell peppers	

1) Heat a small, heavy-based pan and dry roast the cumin seeds until they are a touch darker. Remove them from the pan and leave them to cool.
2) Meanwhile, heat the oil in a large skillet over medium heat and cook the onions for 2–3 minutes.
3) Add both types of peppers and stir-fry them for 1–2 minutes.

4) Cover the pan and let the peppers cook for 4 minutes, stirring halfway through this time.

5) Add the chili powder, salt and paneer or halloumi. Stir gently and cook for 2–3 minutes. Remove from the heat.

6) Crush the roasted cumin seeds with a pestle or the back of a wooden spoon and stir into the cheese and peppers. Serve.

Onion Sambar

Serves 4

S ambar is a South Indian lentil dish that, in spite of the fact that it involves using specially prepared spices, is relatively easy to make.

Serve it with plain and simple boiled basmati rice or Coconut Rice (page 123) and a raita (pages 138–145) or a dry-spiced vegetable dish.

1 cup dried split yellow gram
   (tuvar dhal), boiled and
   drained
3¾ cups hot water
1 tablespoon coriander seeds
1 teaspoon cumin seeds
2–3 dried red chilies
10–12 whole black peppercorns
½ teaspoon black mustard
   seeds

2 teaspoons Bengal gram
   (channa dhal)
¼ cup ghee or unsalted butter
2 cups shallots, quartered
1 teaspoon ground turmeric
1 tablespoon tamarind juice or
   1½ tablespoons lime juice
2 tablespoons chopped fresh
   coriander leaves

1) Wash and drain the yellow split gram, then put it into a saucepan together with the hot water, bring to a boil and let it boil, uncovered, for 6–7 minutes. Then reduce the heat, cover the pan and let it simmer gently for 20 minutes.

2) Meanwhile, heat a heavy-based pan and dry roast the spices and Bengal gram until they are just a shade darker. Stir them constantly. Remove them from the heat, let them cool, then grind them in a coffee grinder.

3) In a skillet heat the ghee or butter over medium heat and cook the shallots until they have browned a little.

4) Add the turmeric and ground spices, stir and cook for 30 seconds, then fold the entire contents of the pan into the yellow split gram.

5) Add the tamarind or lime juice and coriander leaves. Remove from the heat and keep the pan tightly covered until you are ready to serve as this keeps the flavors locked in.

Paneer Bhujia
(Spicy Crumbled Cheese)

Serves 4

Serve with any dhal (pages 66–72) and Hot Mushroom or Tarka Rice (pages 125 and 132).

1 teaspoon cumin seeds

3 tablespoons sunflower or
  soya oil

1 large onion, finely chopped

1–2 green chilies, chopped

¼ teaspoon ground turmeric

1 cup grated paneer or Cyprus
  halloumi cheese

1 tablespoon plain yogurt,
  preferably thick

¼–½ teaspoon salt, or to taste

¼–½ teaspoon chili powder

1 tablespoon chopped fresh
  coriander leaves

1) Heat a small, heavy-based pan over medium heat. Dry roast the cumin seeds in it until they are a shade darker. Remove the seeds from the pan, let them cool, then crush them with a pestle or the back of a wooden spoon. Set aside.

2) Heat the oil over medium-high heat in a non-stick skillet and cook the onion for 2–3 minutes. Reduce the heat a little and continue to cook, stirring frequently, for a further 4–5 minutes, or until the onion has browned lightly.

3) Add the chilies and turmeric. Stir for 30 seconds.

4) Add the paneer or halloumi and stir-fry for a minute or 2 before adding the yogurt. Season to taste with salt (use ½ teaspoon with paneer, ¼ teaspoon with halloumi as the latter is salty) and continue to stir-fry for 3–4 minutes.

5) Add the chili powder and roasted, crushed cumin seeds and stir them in before adding the coriander leaves. Stir once more, remove from the heat and serve.

Cook's Note

Spoon the cheese mixture onto one side of a hot chapatti, put some chopped tomatoes, cucumber and crisp lettuce on top, then roll it up and serve with a soup for a sustaining meal.

Paneer and Potato Curry (Cheese and Potato Curry)

Serves 4

Serve this dish with plain boiled basmati rice or warmed pita or naan and a raita (pages 138–145).

4 tablespoons sunflower or
  soya oil

1 large onion, finely chopped

1-inch cube gingerroot, peeled
  and grated

4 large garlic cloves, minced

1½ tablespoons dhanna jeera
  powder

1 teaspoon ground cumin

½ teaspoon ground turmeric

1 cup chopped fresh or canned,
  drained tomatoes

2 cups cubed potatoes (2-inch
  cubes)

½–1 teaspoon salt

2½ cups hot water

2 cups cubed paneer or Cyprus
  halloumi cheese (2-inch
  cubes)

3 green chilies, 2 left whole, 1
  seeded and sliced lengthwise

1 teaspoon garam masala

2 tablespoons chopped fresh
  coriander leaves

1) In a saucepan heat the oil over medium heat and, stirring frequently, cook the onion, ginger and garlic for 6–7 minutes, until the onion has caramelized and turned golden brown.

2) Add the dhanna jeera, cumin and turmeric. Stir and cook for 1 minute.

3) Add the tomatoes, stir and cook for 3–4 minutes, then reduce the heat slightly and cook for a further 2–3 minutes.

4) Add the potatoes, salt (1 teaspoon if you are using paneer, ½ teaspoon if you are using halloumi as the latter is salty) and the hot water. Bring to a boil, cover the pan, reduce the heat to low and simmer for 10 minutes.

5) Add the paneer or halloumi and whole and sliced chilies. Cover the pan once more and simmer for 10–15 minutes, or until the potatoes are tender.

6) Add the garam masala and fresh coriander, cook for 1 or 2 minutes, then it is ready to serve.

side Dishes

No dish in this section will take you longer than 25 minutes to cook—in fact, some will take only 10 minutes. You need to allow yourself some preparation time, though, and I find that 10–15 minutes is usually sufficient.

Spending a little time and effort on creating wholesome, tasty meals is something I enjoy doing, but I do not like spending *too* much time in the kitchen, so I utilize every few minutes where a dish is taking care of itself to get things ready for the next. Then I find that I have the time to see something good on TV or sit down with that article in a magazine I have set aside to read later and still eat well into the bargain!

The quantities given in the recipes for the side dishes here are generally enough for four people. Note, too, that if you make a recipe and some is left over, Indian dishes keep very well for four to five days in the fridge (just make sure that when you re-heat, it is piping hot all the way through). Indeed, I often cook three or four dishes at a time and put them in the fridge. That way, every evening, I just cook the staples and perhaps make a fresh salad or raita. You can then use the dishes you have made to create a variety of combinations. "Don't work hard, just work clever" is my motto in the kitchen!

Cabbage with Peas

Serves 4

Here you can enjoy the fresh, natural taste of crisp, green cabbage as subtle flavors are used to create this simple but sensational dish. It is delicious served with a bowl of any dhal you like (pages 66–72) and hot, fluffy basmati rice.

3 tablespoons sunflower or
   soya oil
1 large onion, finely sliced
2–3 fresh green chilies, seeded
   and chopped
1-inch cube gingerroot peeled
   and cut into julienne strips

½ teaspoon ground turmeric
1½ lbs finely chopped
   (shredded) green cabbage
1 teaspoon salt, or to taste
1 cup frozen peas
2 tablespoons chopped fresh
   coriander leaves

1) Heat the oil over medium heat in a large pan. Add the onion, chilies and ginger and stir-fry for 4–5 minutes, then reduce the heat slightly. Stir-fry for a further 5–6 minutes, or until the onion has browned lightly.

2) Stir in the turmeric, then add the cabbage and salt. Increase the heat slightly and stir the cabbage until turmeric colors it evenly. Reduce the heat to low, cover and cook for 5 minutes. Remove the lid and sprinkle in the water that has collected on it.

3) Add the peas and stir, mixing them in thoroughly. Cover the pan and cook for 7–8 minutes.

4) Stir in the coriander leaves, remove from the heat and serve.

South Indian Vegetable Curry

Serves 4

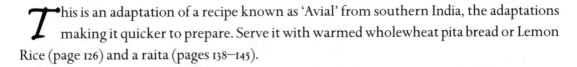

*T*his is an adaptation of a recipe known as 'Avial' from southern India, the adaptations making it quicker to prepare. Serve it with warmed wholewheat pita bread or Lemon Rice (page 126) and a raita (pages 138–145).

1½ cups peeled and cubed potatoes (2-inch cubes)	1 tablespoon sunflower or soya oil
1 cup cut green beans	10–12 dried curry leaves
1 cup scraped and cubed carrots (2-inch cubes)	½ teaspoon crushed dried chilies
2 cups hot water	1 teaspoon ground cumin
½ lb eggplant	1 teaspoon ground coriander
½ cup coconut milk powder	½ teaspoon ground turmeric
1 teaspoon salt, or to taste	

1) Put all the vegetables except the eggplant in a large pan and add 1¼ cups of the hot water. Bring to a boil, then reduce the heat a little, cover the pan and cook for 5 minutes.

2) Meanwhile, peel and quarter the eggplant lengthwise and cut the quarters into 2-inch pieces. Rinse them and add to the vegetables in the pan.

3) Blend the coconut milk powder with the remainder of the hot water and add to the vegetables, along with the salt. Heat until it is gently simmering, then cover the pan and cook for 6–7 minutes.

4) Heat the oil in a small saucepan over medium heat and add the curry leaves and crushed chilies. Follow these quickly with the cumin, coriander and turmeric. Stir-fry the spices for 15–20 seconds, then pour the entire contents of the pan over the vegetables. Stir to distribute the spices evenly, then remove the pan from the heat and serve.

Bombay Potatoes

Serves 4

Bombay Potato is not actually an Indian dish! However, as it is so popular in the West, I decided to team this up with soft rolls, toasted in butter, to create a dish similar to the famous Bombay street snack known as Pao-Bhaji. There vegetables are added to the potatoes, too. Pao (bread) Bhaji (dry, spiced vegetables) is a delicious snack for which a special spice mix (pao-bhaji masala) is available in Indian stores. You can, however, cook this delicious potato dish and achieve an authentic flavor using the ingredients given below. It tastes wonderful with naan or chapattis and a bowl of lentils or chickpeas (garbanzos).

4 tablespoons sunflower or
  soya oil
½ teaspoon black mustard
  seeds
1 teaspoon cumin seeds
1 large onion, finely chopped
1-inch cube gingerroot, peeled
  and grated
4 large garlic cloves, minced
¾ cup chopped canned
  tomatoes with juice

1–1½ teaspoons chili powder
4½ cups cubed potatoes
  (1-inch cubes)
1 teaspoon salt, or to taste
15–20 dried curry leaves
2 cups hot water
1 teaspoon garam masala
8 soft rolls
½ cup butter

1) In a saucepan heat the oil over medium heat. When it is quite hot, but not smoking, add the mustard seeds, followed by the cumin seeds.
2) Add the onion and stir-fry for 3–4 minutes.

3) Add the ginger and garlic and continue to cook for a further 3–4 minutes.

4) Add the tomatoes and chili powder and cook for 2–3 minutes.

5) Add the potatoes, salt, curry leaves and hot water. Bring to a boil, then reduce the heat, cover and simmer gently for 12–15 minutes, or until the potatoes are tender. They should be quite mushy.

6) Stir in the garam masala and remove the pan from the heat.

7) Melt the butter in a skillet and cook the cut surface of the rolls until they have toasted and are crisp. The amount of butter you use depends on how you feel about your waistline—from what I have seen, they don't worry about theirs in Bombay!

Cauliflower Korma

Serves 4

<img style decorative divider>

*A*ll you need with this is your favorite bread and a raita (pages 138–145) for a perfect light meal.

4½ cups bite-sized cauliflower
   florets
⅔ cup light cream
1 cup salted, roasted cashews
¼ cup ghee or unsalted butter
4 green cardamom pods
two 2-inch pieces of cassia bark
   or cinnamon sticks, halved

4 whole cloves
1 large onion, finely sliced
1–2 green chilies, sliced
   diagonally
¾ teaspoon salt, or to taste
⅔ cup hot water
1½ tablespoons lime juice

1) In a saucepan cook the cauliflower in boiling water for just 2 minutes, then drain off the water and set aside.

2) Put the cream and cashews in a blender and blend until the nuts are roughly chopped and mixed into the cream.

3) Melt the ghee or butter in a skillet over a medium heat. Split the top of each cardamom pod (to release their flavor) and cook them with the pieces of cassia bark or cinnamon sticks and the cloves for 15–20 seconds.

4) Add the onion and chilies and cook until the onion has browned lightly.

5) Add the cauliflower and salt and pour in the hot water. Mix well, cover the pan and cook for 2–3 minutes.

6) Add the cream and cashew mixture and stir gently until the cauliflower is well coated. Cook, uncovered, for 2–3 minutes.

7) Stir in the lime juice, then remove the pan from the heat and serve.

Cauliflower and Broccoli with Whole Spices

Serves 4

Serve this with Hot and Spicy Quorn or Tarka Dhal (pages 60 and 70) and plain rice.

3 tablespoons sunflower or
   soya oil
½ teaspoon black mustard
   seeds
½ teaspoon cumin seeds
½–1 teaspoon crushed dried
   chilies
2½ cups bite-sized cauliflower
   florets

2½ cups bite-sized broccoli
   florets
1 teaspoon salt, or to taste
2 tablespoons water
2 tablespoons shredded
   coconut, ground in a coffee
   grinder

1) In a saucepan heat the oil over medium heat until it is quite hot, but not smoking. Add the mustard seeds and, as soon as they crackle, add the cumin seeds then the crushed chilies. Allow them to sizzle for 5–10 seconds.

2) Add the vegetables and salt, stir, then sprinkle the water evenly over the vegetables. Reduce the heat to low, cover the pan and cook for 6–8 minutes, stirring halfway through cooking. When you lift the lid to stir, tilt it so that the water collected in-

side can fall back into the pan. The vegetables need moisture to cook, and yet you want them to retain a crisp texture, so this little bit of water does the job very well.

3) When the vegetables are tender, add the ground coconut and stir until all the moisture is absorbed. The vegetables will be coated with the spices and the coconut. Serve.

Peppers with Besan

Serves 4

A seriously delicious dish with a lovely, nutty taste *and* it takes less than 10 minutes to cook! Serve it with any dhal you like (pages 66–72) and Coconut Rice (page 123).

3 tablespoons sunflower or
   soya oil
½ teaspoon black mustard
   seeds
1 teaspoon cumin seeds
2 green bell peppers, seeded
   and cubed
2 red bell peppers, seeded and
   cubed

½ teaspoon ground turmeric
½ teaspoon chili powder
½ teaspoon garam masala
½ teaspoon salt, or to taste
2 tablespoons besan (gram
   flour), sifted

1) Heat the oil over medium heat in a large, shallow pan. When it is quite hot, but not smoking, throw in the mustard seeds, following these with the cumin seeds.
2) Add the peppers and the remaining ingredients, except the besan. Increase the heat slightly and stir-fry the peppers for 4–5 minutes.
3) Sprinkle the besan all over the vegetables and stir-fry for a further minute. Then you are ready to serve.

Cauliflower with Sesame Seeds

Serves 4

For a great-tasting combination, try this dish with Onion Sambar or Tarka Dhal (pages 75 and 70) and boiled rice. You can also use it as a filling for croissants and serve with Lemon and Lentil Soup (page 4).

3 tablespoons sunflower or soya oil	2 tablespoons shredded coconut
½ teaspoon black mustard seeds	2 tablespoons sesame seeds
½ teaspoon cumin seeds	1 teaspoon salt, or to taste
2–3 large garlic cloves, minced	½ teaspoon ground turmeric
1–2 fresh green chilies, chopped	3 cups bite-sized cauliflower florets
2 cups peeled and cubed potatoes (1-inch cubes)	

1) Heat the oil over medium heat in a large, non-stick skillet. When it is hot, add the mustard seeds. As soon as they pop, add the cumin seeds, then the garlic and chilies. Stir-fry until the garlic browns slightly.

2) Add the potatoes and mix well. Reduce the heat to low, cover and cook for 5 minutes.

3) Meanwhile, heat a small, heavy pan over medium heat for 1–2 minutes. Reduce the heat to low and add the coconut and sesame seeds. Dry roast them together, stirring constantly, for 1–2 minutes, until they have turned golden brown. Remove them from the pan and allow to cool.

4) Add the salt, turmeric and cauliflower to the potatoes, increase the heat a little and cook for 1–2 minutes, stirring constantly. Reduce the heat to low again, cover the pan and cook for 7–8 minutes.

5) Grind the dry roasted coconut and sesame seeds in a coffee grinder until you have a smooth mixture. The natural oils in these ingredients will make the mixture cling to the sides of the grinder. When this happens, switch off the grinder, scrape the mixture together and down from the sides with a teaspoon and resume grinding. Stir this ground mixture into the potato and cauliflower, increase the heat slightly and cook for 1–2 minutes, stirring constantly. Remove from the heat and serve.

Mint and Coriander Eggplant

Serves 4

Soft and succulent pieces of eggplant with fresh herbs are a real treat as a side dish or on hot buttered toast as a snack or with Hearty Vegetable Soup (page 5) for lunch. Otherwise, try it with plain basmati rice and Onion Sambar (page 75).

1½ lbs eggplant

3 tablespoons sunflower or soya oil

1 teaspoon cumin seeds

4 garlic cloves, minced

1–2 fresh red chilies, sliced

½ teaspoon ground turmeric

1 teaspoon salt, or to taste

2 tablespoons water

3 tablespoons chopped fresh coriander leaves

3 tablespoons chopped fresh mint leaves

1) Cut the eggplant lengthwise into 4 slices. Cut the slices crosswise into 2-inch strips and soak them in salted water while you get the other ingredients ready, then drain and rinse them and pat them dry with paper towels.

2) Heat the oil in a skillet over medium heat and add the cumin seeds, garlic and chilies. Cook until the garlic begins to brown.

3) Stir in the turmeric, then add the eggplant and salt. Stir-fry for 1–2 minutes, then reduce the heat. Sprinkle the water over the contents of the pan, cover it and cook gently for 8–10 minutes, stirring and turning the pieces of eggplant at least twice during this time.

4) Add the fresh coriander and mint, stir and cover once more. Cook gently for 5–8 minutes, stirring halfway through this time. Then remove from the heat and serve.

Mushrooms with Peas

Serves 4

A mouthwatering dish for mushroom bhaji fans! If you don't like peas, just leave them out. Either way, served with warmed pita, naan or plain rice and a bowl of dhal (pages 66–72), this is delicious.

4 tablespoons sunflower or soya oil	2 teaspoons ground coriander
1 medium onion, finely chopped	½ teaspoon paprika
½-inch cube gingerroot, peeled and grated	7 tablespoons water
2 green chilies, seeded and chopped	2½ cups closed-cap mushrooms, quartered
½ teaspoon ground turmeric	1 cup frozen peas
1 teaspoon ground cumin	¾ teaspoon salt, or to taste
	1 tablespoon tomato paste
	2 tablespoons chopped fresh coriander leaves

1) In a large skillet heat the oil over medium heat and cook the onion, ginger and chilies for 5–6 minutes, until the onion has softened, but not browned.

2) Add the spices, stir-fry them for 30 seconds, then add 2 tablespoons of the water. Continue cooking, stirring constantly, for a further minute or so, then add 2 more tablespoons of the water. Stir and cook until oil begins to come to the surface of the spice paste.

3) Add the mushrooms, peas, salt and tomato paste blended with the remaining water. Stir and mix well, reduce the heat, cover the pan and simmer gently for 8–10 minutes, stirring halfway through this time.
4) Stir in the coriander leaves, remove from the heat and serve.

Mixed Vegetable Bhaji

Serves 4

Serve with a bread of your choosing and Chickpeas (Garbanzos) in Coconut Milk (page 49) or a dhal (pages 66–72).

3 tablespoons sunflower or soya oil	1 teaspoon ground cumin
½ teaspoon black mustard seeds	½ teaspoon ground turmeric
3–4 garlic cloves, crushed	½ teaspoon chili powder
1½ cups finely chopped carrots	1 teaspoon salt
2¼ cups finely chopped green beans	1 tablespoon besan (gram flour), sifted
2 cups finely chopped potatoes	4 spring onions (scallions), both green and white parts, trimmed and chopped
1 teaspoon ground coriander	

1) In a saucepan heat the oil over medium heat and add the mustard seeds. As soon as they pop, add the garlic and cook until lightly browned.

2) Add all the vegetables except the spring onions (scallions) and increase the heat to high. Stir-fry them for 5 minutes.

3) Mix the coriander, cumin, turmeric, chili powder, salt and besan together in a small bowl, then sprinkle the mixture evenly over the vegetables. Reduce the heat, cover the pan and cook gently for 5 minutes.

4) Add the spring onions (scallions), stir and cook for 2–3 minutes, then remove from the heat and serve.

Cook's Note

Use any leftover mixture in toasted sandwiches and serve with a soup—delicious.

New Potatoes with Mushrooms

Serves 4

New potatoes are best with a pat of butter and some mint, true, but I cook them in all sorts of different ways and they taste great whatever I do to them! Buy the potatoes loose and choose the smallest ones to make this sensational recipe.

Simply serve it with any bread you like and a raita (pages 138–145).

½ lb small new potatoes	⅔ cup milk
¼ cup ghee or unsalted butter	4 cups large, flat mushrooms, quartered
1 medium onion, finely chopped	¾ teaspoon salt, or to taste
2–3 garlic cloves, minced	⅔ cup heavy cream
1 teaspoon paprika	2 tablespoons ground almonds
1 tablespoon ground coriander	1 tablespoon lemon juice
½–1 teaspoon chili powder	

1) Scrub the potatoes under running water and then cook them in boiling water until they are tender.
2) Meanwhile, in a saucepan melt the ghee or butter gently and sauté the onion in it for 3–4 minutes.
3) Add the garlic, paprika, coriander and chili powder. Stir and cook for 1 minute.
4) Add half the milk and increase the heat a little. Stir and cook until the milk evaporates. Repeat this process with the remaining milk.

5) Add the mushrooms, stir well and cover the pan. Reduce the heat and cook gently for 8–10 minutes.

6) Add the salt, cream, potatoes and ground almonds. Cover the pan once more and cook for 3–4 minutes.

7) Stir in the lemon juice, remove from the heat and serve.

Stir-Fried Sweet Corn with Peppers

Serves 4

Serve this dish with naan or chapattis accompanied by Paneer and Potato Curry or Egg and Potato Curry (pages 79 and 53).

3 tablespoons sunflower or
  soya oil
1 teaspoon cumin seeds
1 bunch spring onions
  (scallions), chopped, both
  green and white parts
1 cup green bell pepper, cubed
½ teaspoon ground turmeric
½–1 teaspoon chili powder

2 cups frozen or canned sweet
  corn
¾ teaspoon salt, or to taste
½ cup warm water
1 tablespoon chapatti flour
  (atta)
2 teaspoons lemon juice
2 tablespoons chopped fresh
  coriander leaves

1) Heat the oil in a large skillet or wok over medium heat. When it is hot, add the cumin seeds. As they start crackling, add the spring onions (scallions) and stir-fry for 1 or 2 minutes.
2) Add the pepper, increase the heat slightly and continue to stir-fry for a further minute or so.
3) Add the turmeric, chili powder and sweet corn and stir-fry for 2–3 minutes.
4) Add the salt and water, stirring them in.
5) Sprinkle the chapatti flour evenly over the vegetables, stir and cook for about a minute, then add the lemon juice and coriander leaves. Stir, remove from the heat and serve.

Spicy French Fries

Serves 4

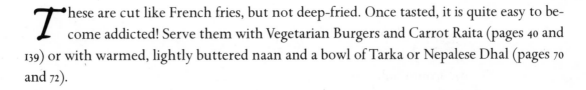

*T*hese are cut like French fries, but not deep-fried. Once tasted, it is quite easy to become addicted! Serve them with Vegetarian Burgers and Carrot Raita (pages 40 and 139) or with warmed, lightly buttered naan and a bowl of Tarka or Nepalese Dhal (pages 70 and 72).

4 tablespoons sunflower or
  soya oil
1 teaspoon black mustard seeds
3 large garlic cloves, minced
4½ cups chopped, French fry-
  style, potatoes

½ teaspoon chili powder, or to
  taste
1 teaspoon salt, or to taste

1) Heat the oil over medium heat in a non-stick skillet. When it is hot, but not smoking, add the mustard seeds and, as soon as they pop, add the garlic. Stir-fry until the garlic has browned lightly.

2) Add the potatoes, chili powder and salt. Stir and cook for 2–3 minutes, reduce the heat slightly and cover the pan. Cook for 5 minutes, increase the heat to medium again, stir and cover the pan once more. Cook for a further 3–4 minutes, then remove the lid and continue to cook, stirring frequently, until the potatoes have browned lightly and are tender. Then, remove from the heat and serve.

Pumpkin Curry

Serves 4

*T*his curry is good served with Tarka Rice (page 132) and a raita (pages 138–145).

¾ cup coconut milk power

2½ cups hot water

2¼ cups peeled and cubed
   pumpkin or butternut
   squash (2-inch cubes)

1 cup peeled and cubed potatoes (2-inch cubes)

1¼ teaspoons salt, or to taste

12–15 dried curry leaves

3–4 green chilies, sliced length-

wise, seeded if wished

2 tablespoons sunflower or
   soya oil

4 large garlic cloves, minced

2 teaspoons ground coriander

1 teaspoon ground cumin

½ teaspoon ground turmeric

1 tablespoon besan (gram
   flour), sifted

1½ tablespoons lime juice

1) Blend the coconut milk powder with the hot water and put it into a saucepan with the ingredients in the list up to and including the green chilies. Heat gently until it is just simmering (it is important to heat it gently; otherwise, the coconut milk will curdle). Cover the pan and continue to simmer very gently for 10 minutes, removing the lid after 5 minutes and stirring once or twice.

2) Heat the oil in a saucepan over medium heat and cook the garlic until it has browned.

3) Add the spices and cook for 30–40 seconds, then stir into the vegetables.

4) Blend the besan with a little water and add this to the vegetables together with the lime juice. Simmer gently for 2–3 minutes, then remove from the heat and serve.

Spinach with Potatoes

Serves 4

*I*love fresh spinach, but if you do not have the time to wash and chop it, use frozen leaf spinach but not puréed spinach, which is not suitable.

Serve with warmed naan, pita or boiled rice and Nepalese Dhal (page 72).

4 tablespoons sunflower or soya oil	4½ cups peeled and cubed potatoes (1-inch cubes)
½ teaspoon black mustard seeds	1 teaspoon salt, or to taste
½ teaspoon cumin seeds	1 teaspoon ground turmeric
1–2 dried red chilies, chopped	1 tablespoon ground coriander
1 medium onion, finely sliced	1 teaspoon ground cumin
3 large garlic cloves, minced	4 cups chopped fresh spinach (see above)
1 green chili, chopped, seeded if wished	

1) Heat the oil in a large, non-stick pan over medium heat. When it is quite hot, but not smoking, add the mustard seeds. As soon as they pop, add the cumin seeds, followed by the red chilies. Let them sizzle for 5–10 seconds.

2) Add the onion, garlic and green chili. Stir-fry them together for 5 minutes, reducing the heat slightly halfway through.

3) Add the potatoes and increase the heat a little. Stir-fry for 5 minutes, then reduce the heat slightly, cover and cook for 3–4 minutes, stirring halfway through. The potatoes and onions should be nicely browned at this point.

4) Stir in the salt and spices. Reduce the heat to low, cover the pan and cook the potatoes gently for 8–10 minutes, stirring halfway through.

5) Add half the spinach and increase the heat a little. Stir until the leaves wilt, then add the remaining spinach. Stir until the leaves wilt, then reduce the heat to low, cover the pan and cook for 6–7 minutes. Stir once or twice during this time.

6) Remove the lid and increase the heat a little, then cook for 3–4 minutes, or until the juices from the spinach have evaporated. Stir frequently during this time, then remove from the heat and serve.

Stuffed Zucchini

Serves 4

Serve this as a side dish with any rice dish you like or bread and a dhal (pages 66–72) or with a soup and hot, buttered rolls.

4 large zucchini

¼ cup unsalted butter

1 small onion, minced

2 green chilies, finely chopped, seeded if desired

¾ cup grated cheddar or other flavorful cheese

2 tablespoons chopped fresh coriander

salt and freshly ground black pepper, to taste

1) Halve the zucchini lengthwise and take a thin slice off the bottom of each half so that they sit upright. Scoop out or scrape off the soft centers of the zucchini halves. Finely chop half of this tender flesh, setting it aside, and discard the remainder.

2) Melt the butter gently over medium heat and use some of it to brush the zucchini halves inside and out.

3) Place the zucchini halves in the bottom of a broiler pan—the grid removed and the bottom of the pan lined with lightly greased foil.

4) In a skillet cook the onion and chilies in the remaining melted butter for 3–4 minutes.

5) Stir in the chopped zucchini flesh, then remove the pan from the heat and let it cool slightly.

6) Meanwhile, heat the broiler until it has reached medium heat. Mix the onion, chili and zucchini mixture with the cheese and fresh coriander and season to taste with salt and pepper. Divide the mixture equally between the zucchini halves and press it down to fill the hollows firmly. Broil the stuffed zucchini for 6–8 minutes, or until browned, then serve.

Stir-Fried Broccoli with Cauliflower

Serves 4

*T*his is delicious with Tarka Rice and Spicy Green Lentils (pages 132 and 59).

3 tablespoons sunflower or soya oil	1 tablespoon besan (gram flour), sifted
4 large garlic cloves, minced	1 teaspoon salt, or to taste
2 fresh red chilies, thickly sliced	1 teaspoon garam masala
2½ cups bite-sized cauliflower florets	1 teaspoon ground cumin
2½ cups bite-sized broccoli florets	

1) Heat the oil in a large, shallow pan over a medium heat and cook the garlic and red chilies for 30 seconds.
2) Add the vegetables and increase the heat slightly. Stir-fry for 3–4 minutes, or until the vegetables begin to brown a little.
3) Reduce the heat to low, mix the remaining ingredients together, then sprinkle them evenly over the vegetables. Cover the pan and cook for 5 minutes.
4) Remove the lid and sprinkle about a tablespoon of water over the vegetables. Stir it in, cover the pan and cook for 2–3 minutes or until the vegetables are tender. Then, remove the pan from the heat and serve.

Rutabaga Bhaji

Serves 4

Grated rutabaga, cooked briefly in a lightly flavored oil, makes an interesting change, and the pungency of chili and the nuttiness of mustard seeds of this recipe complement the slightly sweet taste of rutabaga very well.

Plain rice and Lentils with Green Beans (page 62) are very good accompaniments for this dish.

3 tablespoons sunflower or
 soya oil
½ teaspoon black mustard
 seeds
¼ teaspoon fenugreek seeds
4 large garlic cloves, minced

½ teaspoon crushed chilies
2½ cups grated rutabaga
1 teaspoon salt, or to taste
2 tablespoons chopped fresh
 coriander

1) Heat the oil in a shallow pan over medium heat. When the oil is quite hot, but not smoking, add the mustard seeds.

2) As soon as the mustard seeds pop, add the fenugreek seeds, followed by the garlic. Cook until the garlic has browned slightly.

3) Stir in the crushed chilies then add the rutabaga and salt. Stir to mix well and cook for 2–3 minutes, stirring. Reduce the heat, cover and cook gently for 5–6 minutes.

4) Stir in the coriander, remove from the heat and serve.

Vegetable Korma

Serves 4

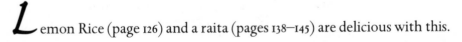

*L*emon Rice (page 126) and a raita (pages 138–145) are delicious with this.

¼ cup ghee or unsalted butter

4 green cardamom pods

½ teaspoon royal cumin (shahi jeera)

1 large onion, finely chopped

1-inch cube gingerroot, peeled and grated

4–5 garlic cloves, minced

2 teaspoons ground coriander

½ teaspoon chili powder

¼ teaspoon ground turmeric

2 cups peeled and cubed potatoes (2-inch cubes)

1¼ cups very thickly sliced carrots

2 cups warm water

⅔ cup milk

½ cup roughly broken cashew nuts

2 cups cubed eggplant (2-inch cubes)

1¼ cups bite-sized cauliflower florets

1 teaspoon salt, or to taste

1) In a saucepan heat the ghee or butter gently over medium-low heat.

2) Peel back the tops of the cardamom pods very slightly and cook them together with the royal cumin for 15–20 seconds.

3) Add the onion and cook for 3–4 minutes, stirring frequently.

4) Add the ginger and garlic and continue to cook until the onions have softened, but not browned.

5) Add the spices, stir and cook for 30–40 seconds.

6) Add the potatoes, carrots and warm water. Bring to a boil, reduce the heat a little and cover the pan. Cook for 5–6 minutes.

7) Meanwhile, put the milk and cashews in a blender and process until you have a smooth mixture. Add this to the vegetables, together with the eggplant, cauliflower and salt, cover the pan and cook for 5–6 minutes. Stir and turn the vegetables once during this time, then remove from the heat and serve.

Vegetables with Besan

Serves 4

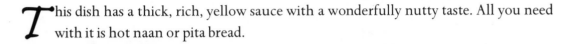

*T*his dish has a thick, rich, yellow sauce with a wonderfully nutty taste. All you need with it is hot naan or pita bread.

3 tablespoons sunflower or
    soya oil
½ teaspoon black mustard
    seeds
1 teaspoon cumin seeds
12–15 dried curry leaves
1–2 green chilies, chopped
2 cups peeled and cubed
    potatoes (2-inch cubes)
2½ cups bite-sized cauliflower
    florets

½ cup chopped canned
    tomatoes with their juice
1 teaspoon salt, or to taste
¼–½ teaspoon chili powder
½ teaspoon ground turmeric
½ cup besan (gram flour), sifted
⅔ cup cold water
1¼ cups hot water

1) In a saucepan heat the oil over medium heat and add the mustard seeds. As soon as they pop, add the cumin seeds, curry leaves and green chilies.

2) Add the potatoes and increase the heat. Stir-fry the potatoes until they brown a little, then reduce the heat, cover the pan and cook for 2–3 minutes.

3) Add the cauliflower and increase the heat. Sauté the vegetables for 2–3 minutes.

4) Reduce the heat and add the remaining ingredients except the besan and water. Stir and cook for 1 or 2 minutes.

5) Blend the besan with the cold water and add this mixture to the vegetables. Stir and cook for a minute before pouring in the hot water. Cook for 2–3 minutes, stirring gently. Then, remove from the heat and serve.

Spicy Sweet Potatoes

Serves 4

*O*nion Sambar or Spicy Green Lentils and Cumin Rice (pages 75, 59 and 122) would be great with this.

3 cups peeled, bite-sized pieces of sweet potatoes	6–8 fenugreek seeds
4 tablespoons sunflower or soya oil	6 large garlic cloves, minced
½ teaspoon black mustard seeds	½–1 teaspoon chili powder
1 teaspoon cumin seeds	½ teaspoon ground turmeric
	1 teaspoon salt, or to taste
	¼ cup besan (gram flour)

1) Soak the potatoes in cold water for about 10 minutes. Then drain and rinse them well.

2) Heat the oil in a large skillet, preferably non-stick, over medium heat. When it is quite hot, but not smoking, throw in the mustard seeds, then the cumin and fenugreek seeds and the garlic. Stir-fry until the garlic has browned a little.

3) Stir in the chili powder and turmeric and add the potatoes and salt. Stir-fry for 2–3 minutes, then cover the pan and cook for 3–4 minutes. Then, remove the lid, increase the heat and cook, stirring frequently, for 3–4 minutes more, or until the potatoes are tender and have browned lightly.

4) Sprinkle the besan evenly over the potatoes, stir and cook for 1–2 minutes before removing the pan from the heat and serving.

Rice and Bread

Rice and bread are the staple foods in India. About 10,0000 different varieties of rice are grown in India. Because of its unique natural aroma, normally I prefer to use the traditional basmati rice for cooking pulao dishes. I have, however, used easy-cook basmati rice in some of the pulaos in this chapter. It is easy to handle and does not need to be presoaked. I have been delighted with the results.

As far as bread is concerned, we have to rely on the supermarkets and specialty shops (see p. xiii for mail order information) when we are busy! They all have an excellent selection of breads—so much so, it is hardly worth making your own, especially when you are pushed for time. Reheating them successfully is simple if you follow the tips I give you in the recipes.

Baby Vegetable Pulao

Serves 4

A raita such as Tomato and Cucumber, Spinach or Pumpkin (pages 145, 143 or 141) complements this pulao well, as does Tarka Dhal (page 70). Poppadoms are excellent with a raita and pulao.

1½ cups easy-cook basmati rice
⅓ cup ghee or unsalted butter
1 large onion, finely sliced
4 green cardamom pods, the
   top of each pod split
two 2-inch pieces cassia bark or
   cinnamon sticks, halved
4 cloves
½-inch cube gingerroot, peeled
   and grated
3 large garlic cloves, minced

1–2 green chilies, seeded and
   chopped
1 tablespoon dhanna jeera
   powder
½ teaspoon ground turmeric
¾ cup baby carrots, halved
1 cup baby corn, halved
¾ cup baby green beans, halved
1 teaspoon salt, or to taste
¾ cup coconut milk powder
2¼ cups hot water

1) Wash the rice 2–3 times in cold water and leave to drain in a colander.
2) In a skillet heat the ghee or butter over medium heat and cook the onion in it for 8–9 minutes, until it has browned. Lift it with a slotted spoon and press it down with another spoon to remove the excess fat. Drain on paper towels.
3) In the fat remaining in the pan, cook the ingredients in the list up to and including the green chilies for about a minute.

4) Add dhanna jeera powder and turmeric, cook for 30 seconds, then add the vegetables and salt. Stir-fry for 2–3 minutes.

5) Add the rice, stir and fry for 2–3 minutes.

6) Blend the coconut milk powder with the hot water and add this mixture to the rice and vegetables together with half the onions. Bring to a boil, reduce the heat, cover the pan and simmer gently for 15–17 minutes.

7) Remove from the heat and leave the pan undisturbed for 6–7 minutes—this allows the moisture to be absorbed by the rice. Fork through the pulao and serve garnished with the remaining onions.

Chickpea (Garbanzo) Pulao

Serves 4

*L*ettuce and Coconut Sauce or Spinach and Coconut Sauce (pages 150 and 151) are excellent with this pulao, even though they are served cold. Alternatively, serve a raita (pages 138–145) or grilled (broiled) or fried poppadoms.

⅓ cup ghee or unsalted butter

6 green cardamom pods

two 2-inch pieces of cassia bark
   or cinnamon sticks, halved

6 cloves

1 large onion, finely sliced

2 green chilies, seeded and
   chopped

½-inch cube gingerroot, peeled
   and grated

2 large garlic cloves, minced

2 teaspoons ground coriander

1 teaspoon ground cumin

½ teaspoon ground turmeric

1½ cups basmati rice, washed,
   soaked for 15 minutes, and
   drained

1¼ cups canned, drained and
   rinsed chickpeas (garbanzos)

1¼ teaspoons salt, or to taste

2½ cups hot water

¼ cup chopped fresh coriander

1) Heat the ghee or butter over medium heat in a heavy saucepan. Peel the top of each cardamom pod back very slightly and add them to the ghee, together with the cassia bark or cinnamon sticks and cloves. Let them sizzle for 15–20 seconds.

2) Add the onion, green chilies, ginger and garlic. Stir-fry until the onion has caramelized and turned golden brown.

3) Add the spices and cook for a minute, then add the rice, chickpeas (garbanzos) and salt. Stir-fry for 2–3 minutes, then add the hot water and fresh coriander. Bring to a boil, reduce the heat, cover the pan and cook for 10 minutes. Remove from the heat and leave it to stand for 6–7 minutes, so all the liquid can be absorbed. Fluff the rice up with a fork and serve.

Cumin Rice

Serves 4

Cumin-flavored fried rice, using traditional basmati, tastes luxurious even with the simplest curry.

¼ cup ghee or unsalted butter	1 teaspoon salt, or to taste
1 teaspoon cumin seeds	2 cups hot water
2 bay leaves, crumbled	
1½ cups basmati rice, washed and soaked for 15 minutes	

1) Melt the ghee or butter in a non-stick saucepan over medium heat and cook the cumin seeds and bay leaves for 15–20 seconds.

2) Drain the rice, then add it to the pan and fry for 3–4 minutes.

3) Stir in the salt and pour in the hot water. Bring to a boil, reduce the heat, cover the pan and simmer gently for 10 minutes. Do not lift the lid during this time.

4) Remove the pan from the heat and leave it undisturbed for 6–7 minutes, then separate the rice with a fork before serving.

Coconut Rice

Serves 4

Serve with Hot and Spicy Quorn or Spicy Green Lentils (pages 60 and 59) and a raita (pages 138–145) is nice, if you have time.

1½ cups basmati rice	10–12 dried curry leaves
2 tablespoons sunflower or	1 teaspoon salt, or to taste
soya oil	½ cup coconut milk powder
1 teaspoon black mustard seeds	2 cups hot water
1 teaspoon cumin seeds	

1) Rinse the rice at least twice in cold water and let it soak for 15 minutes.
2) Heat the oil in a non-stick saucepan over medium heat. When it is quite hot, but not smoking, add the mustard seeds, closely following these with the cumin seeds and curry leaves. Let them all sizzle for 10–15 seconds.
3) Drain the rice and add it to the pan, together with the salt. Stir-fry for 1–2 minutes.
4) Blend the coconut milk powder with the hot water and add this to the pan. Heat until it is gently simmering, then reduce the heat, cover the pan and let it continue to simmer gently for 12 minutes.
5) Remove the pan from the heat and let it sit for 6–7 minutes so all the liquid is absorbed by the rice. If the rice looks soggy after this time, just leave it a little longer as the rice absorbs coconut milk more slowly than plain water.

Fried Rice with Spring Onions (Scallions)

Serves 4

*T*his is a really useful recipe as you can serve this rice with almost any dish.

1½ cups easy-cook basmati rice
¼ cup ghee or unsalted butter
2 garlic cloves, minced
1 bunch spring onions
   (scallions), trimmed and
   both green and white parts
   chopped

2 vegetable stock (bouillon)
   cubes
2½ cups hot water
salt, to taste

1) Rinse the rice at least twice in cold water, then leave to drain in a colander.
2) Melt the ghee or butter in a non-stick pan and cook the garlic and spring onions (scallions) for 2–3 minutes.
3) Add the rice and stir-fry for 4–5 minutes.
4) Crumble the stock cubes, sprinkling them over the rice, then pour in the hot water. Add a little salt to taste if you wish. Bring to a boil, then reduce the heat, cover the pan and simmer gently for 15–17 minutes.
5) Remove the pan from the heat and let it sit, undisturbed, for 5–10 minutes before fluffing the rice with a fork and serving.

Hot Mushroom Rice

Serves 4

Easy-cook basmati rice works wonderfully in this recipe. Although manufacturer's instructions say that it is not necessary to rinse the rice, I find it works better if you do rinse it and leave it to drain for a few minutes in a colander.

¼ cup ghee or unsalted butter

4 garlic cloves, minced

½-inch cube gingerroot, peeled and grated

2–3 green chilies, seeded and cut into julienne strips

½ teaspoon ground turmeric

1½ cups easy-cook basmati rice, rinsed and drained

2 cups sliced closed-cap mushrooms

1 teaspoon salt, or to taste

1 tablespoon chopped fresh coriander leaves

2½ cups hot water

1) In a saucepan heat the ghee or butter over medium heat and cook the garlic, ginger and green chilies for about a minute, or until they have browned.

2) Add the turmeric, rice, mushrooms, salt and coriander leaves. Stir-fry for 2–3 minutes.

3) Pour the hot water into the pan. Bring to a boil, then reduce the heat, cover the pan and simmer gently for 15–17 minutes.

4) Remove the pan from the heat and let it sit undisturbed for 6–7 minutes. Just before serving, fluff the rice with a fork.

Lemon Rice

Serves 4

A delicious and refreshing way to serve basmati rice. Try it with Hot and Spicy Quorn or Nepalese Dhal (pages 60 and 72).

1½ cups basmati rice	1 oz broken cashew nuts
2 tablespoons sunflower or soya oil	¼ teaspoon ground turmeric
1 teaspoon black mustard seeds	1 teaspoon salt, or to taste
10–12 dried curry leaves	2½ cups hot water
	2 tablespoons lemon juice

1) Rinse the rice and soak it for 15 minutes. Then, let it drain in a colander.
2) Heat the oil in a non-stick saucepan over medium heat. When the oil is quite hot, but not smoking, add the mustard seeds, curry leaves and cashews and let them cook for 15–20 seconds.
3) Add the rice, turmeric and salt. Stir-fry the rice for 2–3 minutes, then add the hot water and lemon juice. Stir once, bring to a boil and continue to boil for 2 minutes.
4) Cover the pan tightly, reduce the heat and simmer gently for 10 minutes.
5) Remove the pan from the heat and let it stand, undisturbed, for 6–7 minutes. Fluff the rice with a fork and serve.

Tomato and Coriander Rice

Serves 4

A very tasty and attractive dish for which I have used traditional basmati rice.

1½ cups basmati rice

¼ cup ghee or unsalted butter

1 teaspoon royal cumin (shahi
   jeera)

1 tablespoon tomato paste

1 teaspoon salt, or to taste

2 cups hot water

½ cup chopped fresh coriander
   leaves

1) Rinse the rice at least twice in cold water and leave to soak for 15 minutes. Then drain.

2) In a saucepan heat the ghee or butter over medium heat and cook the royal cumin for 15–20 seconds.

3) Add the rice, tomato paste and salt. Stir-fry for 2–3 minutes.

4) Pour in the hot water, bring to a boil and stir in the coriander leaves. Reduce the heat, cover the pan and simmer gently for 10 minutes.

5) Remove the pan from the heat and let it sit undisturbed for 6–7 minutes before fluffing with a fork and serving.

Lentil Pulao

Serves 4

This recipe is adapted from the Anglo-Indian dish known as kedgeree. I have used yellow lentils (moong dhal) as this is the fastest cooking lentil. Accompanied by a raita (pages 138–145), this is extremely tasty.

1½ cups basmati rice
½ cup dried split yellow lentils
   (moong dhal)
⅓ cup ghee or unsalted butter
1 large onion, finely sliced
two 2-inch piece of cassia bark
   or cinnamon sticks, halved
6 cloves
1–2 green chilies, seeded and
   chopped

½-inch cube gingerroot, peeled
   and grated
2 bay leaves, crumbled
2 teaspoons ground coriander
1¼ teaspoons salt, or to taste
2½ cups hot water
2–3 hard-cooked eggs, quartered lengthwise, to garnish

1) Rinse the rice and lentils together and leave them to drain in a colander.
2) In a saucepan heat the ghee or butter over medium heat and cook the onion, stirring frequently, for 8–9 minutes, until it has browned well. Lift the onion with a slotted spoon and press down with another spoon to remove the excess fat. Leave to drain on paper towels.
3) In the same pan, cook the remaining ingredients except the salt, water and eggs for 15–20 seconds.

4) Add the rice and lentils, salt and half the onions. Stir-fry for 2–3 minutes.

5) Pour in the hot water, bring to a boil, reduce the heat, cover the pan and simmer gently for 10 minutes.

6) Remove the pan from the heat and let it sit, undisturbed, for 6–7 minutes.

7) Fluff the pulao with a fork and serve, garnished with the hard-cooked eggs and the remaining onion.

Paneer Pulao
Cheese and Spiced Rice

Serves 4

*P*aneer is an Indian cheese that is available in all Indian shops. If you cannot get it, use Cyprus halloumi cheese instead, which is sold in most good supermarkets. Use easy-cook basmati rice for speed as well as perfect results.

The ideal accompaniments for this dish are Spinach or Pumpkin Raita (pages 143 and 141) or a sauce, such as Lettuce and Coconut or Spinach and Coconut Sauce (pages 150 and 151).

¼ cup ghee or unsalted butter
6 green cardamom pods
two 2-inch pieces of cassia bark
　or cinnamon sticks, halved
6 whole cloves
1 large onion, finely sliced
1-inch cube gingerroot, peeled
　and grated
2–3 large garlic cloves, crushed
1 teaspoon ground turmeric
1 teaspoon ground cumin
2 teaspoons ground coriander

½ cup canned chopped
　tomatoes with their juice
1½ cups easy-cook basmati rice,
　rinsed
1 teaspoon salt, or to taste
1 cup cubed paneer or Cyprus
　halloumi cheese (1-inch
　cubes)
2½ cups hot water
2 teaspoons chopped fresh
　coriander leaves

1) In a saucepan heat the ghee or butter gently over medium-low heat.

2) Split the top of each cardamom pod and add them to the pan, together with the cassia bark or cinnamon sticks and cloves. Let them sizzle for 15–20 seconds.

3) Add the onion, ginger and garlic, increase the heat slightly and cook, stirring frequently, for 6–7 minutes, or until the onion has browned lightly.

4) Add the spices and stir-fry for 1 minute.

5) Add the tomatoes, stir and cook for 2–3 minutes.

6) Add the rice, salt and paneer or halloumi. Stir gently and cook for 2–3 minutes.

7) Add the hot water and coriander and bring to a boil. Reduce the heat, cover the pan and simmer gently for 15–17 minutes.

8) Remove the pan from the heat and let it sit, undisturbed, for 6–7 minutes. Then, fluff the rice with a fork before serving.

Tarka Rice
(Seasoned Rice)

Serves 4

A "tarka" (which means seasoning) is prepared in hot oil and cooked rice is tossed in it until the rice has heated through. Do make sure you use a non-stick pan for this, otherwise the cooked rice will stick.

This dish goes well with any lentil, bean or vegetable dish.

1½ cups cooked basmati or any easy-cook rice	1 teaspoon cumin seeds
4 cups hot water	2–3 whole, small, dried red chilies
1 tablespoon sunflower or soya oil	10–12 dried curry leaves
½ teaspoon black mustard seeds	½ teaspoon ground turmeric
	½ teaspoon salt, or to taste

1) Rinse the rice 2–3 times in cold water, then let it drain.
2) Put the rice into a saucepan with the hot water and bring to a boil. Then, reduce the heat a little and cook the rice, uncovered, for 10–12 minutes.
3) Drain the rice and rinse it thoroughly under cold running water, then leave it to drain in a colander.
4) Heat the oil over medium heat in a non-stick pan. When it is hot, but not smoking, add the mustard seeds. As soon as they pop, add the remaining ingredients except the salt and rice. Let the spices sizzle for 20–25 seconds.

5) Add the rice and salt, reduce the heat and stir-fry gently until the rice has heated through, coating the rice in the spicy oil. Then, remove from the heat and serve.

Cook's Note

If you really want to save time, cook extra plain, boiled rice whenever you have it on the menu. Then, store it in the fridge or freeze it and you will have some ready to make Tarka Rice.

Hot Tips for Making the Most of Bought Breads

When you are cooking Indian meals in just 30 minutes, you will not have enough time to make bread yourself. This does not mean, however, that you cannot include bread in your menu. Choose from the wide range of breads available in the supermarkets, specialty food shops, or by mail order. If you keep them in the fridge, you can prolong their life by a couple of days and, of course, you can always freeze them. To reheat bread straight from the freezer without drying it out, simply follow the steps below, and read on for other creative ideas.

Reheating frozen naan or pita bread

1. Preheat the broiler to medium (I do not recommend using an oven for reheating when your schedule is tight as preheating an oven takes time—using the broiler is quick and easy).
2. Hold the bread under cold running water for 5–10 seconds, making sure both sides are quite wet.
3. Shake off the excess water and broil until the surface is dry, then turn over and broil the other side until it is just dry; each side will only take about 30 seconds. Take care to turn the bread over just as soon as the water dries up as any overheating will make the bread dry and tough.

If you follow these steps, your bread will be hot, soft and really fluffy. If you like, you can lightly butter the bread on one side after broiling for extra taste.

Reheating ready-cooked chapattis

1. Preheat an iron griddle or other heavy-based skillet over medium heat for a couple of minutes.

2. Brush the pan with a little oil and place the chapatti on it. Cook it for 30–40 seconds, then brush the uncooked side with a little oil, turn it over and cook that side for 30–40 seconds. Repeat for the rest of the chapattis, keeping the cooked ones wrapped in a piece of foil lined with wax paper until you have finished reheating all of them.

To flavor plain naan

1. Hold the naan under cold running water, as in step 2 of Reheating naan or pita above.

2. Heat one side under the broiler until the water dries up, then follow either step 3 or 4.

3. Turn the naan over and sprinkle grated cheddar or other flavorful cheese mixed with chopped fresh coriander (and chopped green chilies, too, if you like) and broil until the cheese has melted. Serve immediately.

4. Alternatively, turn the naan over and brush the uncooked side with a little plain yogurt and sprinkle white poppy seeds or sesame seeds over the top and broil for about a minute. Serve immediately.

To turn plain naan into a substantial meal

1. Heat the naan on one side, moistening it first as described on page 134.

2. Mix finely chopped onion, green chili and fresh coriander leaves with baked beans and spread this mixture on the uncooked side, sprinkle grated cheese over the top and broil gently until the top is bubbling and has browned in places. Serve with a bowl of soup or dhal (pages 66–72).

To transform sliced bread

You can flavor humble sliced bread very quickly the following way.

Cumin and Coriander Bread

For 8–10 slices of bread

You can vary the flavor of this bread by omitting the ground spices and adding a combination of cumin seeds and crushed black peppercorns, onion seeds and a little chili powder, garlic paste and royal cumin—let your creativity go!

6 tablespoons softened butter

1 teaspoon ground cumin

½ teaspoon paprika

1 tablespoon finely chopped fresh coriander

1) Mix all the ingredients together and spread on the sliced bread.
2) Broil them gently until the mixture begins to bubble and brown very slightly.

Raitas and Chutney

The recipes for raitas included here can be served with almost any dish. They are all quick to make, but the ones with cooked vegetables in them will take slightly longer because these need to cool before they can be folded into the yogurt. This can prove useful, though, as you can use this time to prepare something else.

Raitas are lovely when piled on warmed naan. This is not a traditional Indian way to eat them, but they are delicious just the same! You will also find that most of them are really good with Cumin and Coriander Bread (page 136).

Just like raitas, chutneys can accompany and add extra interest to a meal. They are also delicious served with cooked poppadoms or savory biscuits or graham crackers, instead of a dip.

Sweet Corn Raita

Serves 4

1 tablespoon sunflower or soya oil

½ teaspoon black mustard seeds

1 large garlic clove, minced

1 green chili, seeded and chopped

¾ cup frozen or canned sweet corn kernels, drained and rinsed

½ teaspoon salt, or to taste

1 tablespoon water

1 tablespoon finely chopped fresh coriander leaves

1 cup whole milk plain yogurt

1) In a skillet heat the oil over medium heat until it is fairly hot, but not smoking.
2) Add the mustard seeds, then the garlic and green chili. Stir-fry until the garlic has browned lightly.
3) Add the sweet corn and salt, stir and cook until everything is thoroughly mixed together. Then, reduce the heat, sprinkle the water over the vegetables, cover the pan and cook gently for 4–5 minutes.
4) Stir in the coriander leaves, then remove the pan from the heat and leave to cool.
5) In a bowl beat the yogurt with a fork until it is smooth, then stir in the cooked, cooled sweet corn and serve.

Carrot Raita

Serves 4

½ teaspoon cumin seeds	½ teaspoon salt
10 black peppercorns	½ teaspoon sugar
¾ cup whole milk plain yogurt	1 cup grated carrots

1) Heat a small, heavy saucepan or skillet over medium heat and dry roast the cumin seeds and peppercorns together for a minute or so, until they release their aroma. Transfer them to a plate and leave them to cool.

2) In a bowl beat the yogurt with a fork until it is smooth, then add the salt and sugar.

3) Crush the roasted spices with a pestle or place them in a plastic storage bag and crush with a rolling pin. Mix most of the mixture into the yogurt, add the grated carrots, mix thoroughly, then sprinkle the remaining spices over the top.

Mushroom Raita

Serves 4

2 tablespoons butter
2–3 garlic cloves, minced
1 green chili, seeded and
 chopped
2½ cups chopped, closed-cap
 mushrooms

½ teaspoon salt, or to taste
½ teaspoon ground cumin
2 tablespoons chopped fresh
 coriander
1 cup whole milk plain yogurt

1) In a skillet melt the butter and cook the garlic and chili in it gently until the garlic
begins to brown.

2) Add the mushrooms and salt, increase the heat and stir-fry for 5 minutes.

3) Add the cumin and fresh coriander and stir-fry for 15–20 seconds. Then, remove the
pan from the heat and leave to cool.

4) In a bowl beat the yogurt until it is smooth, then stir it into the cooled, cooked
mushrooms.

Pumpkin Raita

Serves 4

1 tablespoon sunflower or
  soya oil
½ teaspoon black mustard
  seeds
2 garlic cloves, minced
1–2 fresh green chilies, seeded
  and chopped
1 teaspoon ground cumin
2 cups peeled and cubed
  pumpkin or butternut
  squash (1-inch cubes)

½ teaspoon salt
1 teaspoon sugar
½ cup whole milk plain yogurt
¼ cup crème fraîche
1 tablespoon finely chopped
  fresh coriander leaves
sprinkling of chili powder, to
  garnish, optional

1) In a saucepan heat the oil over a medium heat and, when it is quite hot, but not smoking, add the mustard seeds. As soon as they pop, add the garlic and let it brown a little.

2) Add the fresh chilies, cumin, pumpkin or butternut squash, salt and sugar. Stir and mix everything together thoroughly, then reduce the heat, sprinkle 2–3 tablespoons of water over the vegetables, cover the pan and simmer gently for 10 minutes, stirring once or twice during this time.

3) Remove the pan from the heat and set aside to cool.

4) In a bowl beat the yogurt and the crème fraîche together until they are well blended.

5) When the pumpkin or squash mixture has cooled, stir it into the yogurt and crème fraîche mixture with the coriander leaves. Sprinkle with a little chili powder, if you wish.

Spinach Raita

Serves 4

1 tablespoon sunflower or soya oil	1–2 green chilies, seeded and chopped
½ teaspoon black mustard seeds	4 cups chopped fresh spinach
½ teaspoon cumin seeds	½ teaspoon salt, or to taste
2 garlic cloves, minced	1 cup whole milk plain yogurt
	1 small red onion, chopped

1) In a saucepan heat the oil over medium heat and, when it is quite hot, but not smoking, throw in the mustard seeds, followed by the cumin seeds, and let them pop for 5–10 seconds.
2) Add the garlic and chilies and stir-fry for 15–20 seconds.
3) Add the spinach and salt, stir and cook until the spinach begins to wilt. Reduce the heat, cover the pan and simmer gently for 5 minutes.
4) Increase the heat, and cook, uncovered, until all the liquid has evaporated. Remove the pan from the heat and leave to cool.
5) In a bowl beat the yogurt until it is smooth and add the cooled, cooked spinach and half the chopped onion. Mix thoroughly and sprinkle the remaining onion on top.

Tomato and Coconut Raita

Serves 4

You may think this a long list of ingredients for a raita, but, really, it is quite quick to make and is truly delicious.

1 tablespoon sunflower, corn or vegetable oil

½ teaspoon black mustard seeds

½ teaspoon cumin seeds

2 garlic cloves, lightly crushed, then chopped

⅓ cup shredded coconut

2⅔ cups skinned and chopped fresh tomatoes

1–2 fresh green chilies, seeded and chopped

1 teaspoon salt, or to taste

1 teaspoon sugar

½ cup plain yogurt

1 tablespoon finely chopped fresh coriander leaves

1) In a saucepan heat the oil over a medium heat and, when it is hot but not smoking, add the mustard seeds. As soon as they pop, add the cumin seeds, followed by the garlic. Stir-fry for 15–20 seconds, or until the garlic has browned a little.

2) Grind the coconut in a coffee mill, then add it and the tomatoes, fresh chilies, salt and sugar to the pan. Reduce the heat slightly, cover and cook for 8–10 minutes, stirring once or twice during that time. Then, remove the pan from the heat and leave to cool.

3) In a bowl beat the yogurt until it is smooth and add the coriander leaves.

4) Stir the cooled, cooked tomato and coconut mixture into the yogurt and serve.

Tomato and Cucumber Raita

Serves 4

¾ cup plain yogurt
½ teaspoon salt
½ teaspoon sugar
½ teaspoon ground cumin
1 tablespoon chopped fresh
   coriander leaves

½ cucumber, coarsely chopped
2 firm, ripe tomatoes, coarsely
   chopped
¼ teaspoon chili powder

1) In a bowl beat the yogurt with a fork until it is smooth.
2) Add the salt, sugar, cumin and coriander leaves, mixing them in thoroughly, then stir in the cucumber and tomatoes.
3) Spoon the raita into a serving bowl and sprinkle the chili powder over the top.

Coriander and Coconut Chutney

Serves 4

⅓ cup shredded coconut
½ cup chopped fresh coriander,
   including the tender stalks
½-inch cube gingerroot, peeled
   and roughly chopped
1 large garlic clove, peeled and
   roughly chopped

1–2 fresh green chilies, seeded
   and chopped
½ teaspoon salt
½ teaspoon sugar
½ cup whole milk plain yogurt
½ cup sour cream

1) Grind the coconut in a coffee grinder until it is powdery and smooth. Do not use a blender or food processor as they will not grind the coconut finely enough.

2) Transfer the coconut to a blender and add the remaining ingredients. Blend until the mixture is smooth.

3) If you have time, chill the chutney for 15–20 minutes before serving. To chill it quickly, you can place it in the freezer for a few minutes.

Summer Sensations

*I*n the West, Indian food is often associated with autumn and winter. As soon as summer says good-bye and autumn sets in, we prepare ourselves for the long, dark evenings of the winter months. Comforting, warming foods of all kinds come to mind, and cooking and serving exciting, spicy dishes during these months can be one way to fight the winter blues.

No one wants to spend much time in the kitchen during the long summer evenings, which are traditionally a time for outdoor activities. The abundance of summer fruits and vegetables makes it easier to serve up light, nutritious meals. These two things naturally combine, explaining why eating al fresco has become so popular.

Don't restrict yourself to eating Indian meals just when it is cold outside—exciting Indian foods can be cooked without much effort all year round! Indeed, the recipes that follow offer just a glimpse of the enormous repertoire of Indian summer dishes. These particular recipes are not common knowledge, even in India! Devised by a small community in southern India (to which I belong through marriage), these recipes are simple and delicious.

I have also created a few quick desserts using summer fruits. After all, a meal does not seem complete without a dessert, and my book would have felt incomplete without these!

Pumpkin Soup

Serves 4

Pumpkins are more easily available in the autumn, in time for Halloween, but some Asian and Caribbean shops have pumpkins all year. If you cannot find a pumpkin, you could use butternut squash.

1¾ cups peeled and roughly chopped pumpkin	1¼ cups hot water
2 green chilies, seeded and chopped	1¼ cups cold water
12–15 dried curry leaves	1 cup whole milk plain yogurt
2 teaspoons peeled and roughly chopped gingerroot	1 teaspoon salt, or to taste
⅓ cup shredded coconut	1 teaspoon sugar
	1 tablespoon lime juice
	1 tablespoon finely chopped fresh coriander leaves

1) Put the pumpkin, chilies, curry leaves, ginger and coconut into a saucepan and add the hot water. Bring to a boil, cover the pan, reduce the heat and simmer gently for 10 minutes, or until the pumpkin is tender.

2) Remove the pan from the heat and let it cool for 5–6 minutes.

3) Purée the pumpkin in a blender. Add the cold water, yogurt, salt and sugar to the blender and blend until the ingredients are well mixed.

4) Add the lime juice and fresh coriander to the blender, blend once more for a few seconds and then either serve the soup at room temperature or chilled.

Seasoned Mango with Coconut

Serves 4

Ripe mangoes, coated with coconut and seasoned with mustard and coriander, make a superb side dish with summer meals. You can serve this instead of a salad with just about anything you fancy. It can also be eaten on its own after a meal instead of a dessert.

4–5 ripe, firm mangoes

2 teaspoons soft brown sugar

¾ teaspoon salt, or to taste

1 tablespoon lime juice

⅓ cup shredded coconut

2 dried red chilies, chopped

1 tablespoon sunflower oil

½ teaspoon black mustard
   seeds

½ teaspoon ground coriander

1) Peel the mangoes and slice off the flesh on either side of the central pit. Slice off the two remaining smaller pieces (I normally enjoy sucking off the flesh left next to the pit at this point!). Chop the mango flesh into bite-sized pieces.

2) Put the mango into a mixing bowl and add the sugar, salt and lime juice. Mix them together well.

3) Grind the coconut and red chilies in a coffee grinder until you have a fine, powdery mixture. Add this to the mango mixture and stir them together until they are evenly distributed.

4) Heat the oil in a small saucepan over a medium heat. When it is hot, but not smoking, add the mustard seeds. As soon as they pop, stir in the coriander, allow them to cook together for 5–10 seconds, then remove the pan from the heat. Pour this spiced oil over the mango mixture and stir them together well. Serve at room temperature or chilled.

Lettuce and Coconut Sauce

Serves 4

A very unusual dish that is served cold. Strange through it may sound, it tastes great with boiled basmati rice. It is also excellent with hot naan or pita bread. Serve Spiced Corn on the Cob (page 36) as a starter (appetizer) if you choose either of these options as your main course.

⅔ cup shredded coconut

2 green chilies, seeded and chopped

2 teaspoons peeled and chopped gingerroot

1¼ cups hot water

2 cups lettuce leaves

1 cup chopped fresh tomatoes

¼ cup plain yogurt

1 tablespoon lime juice

½ teaspoon ground cumin

1 teaspoon salt, or to taste

1) Put the coconut, chilies and ginger into a saucepan and add the hot water. Bring to a boil.

2) Add the lettuce and tomatoes, bring back to a boil, then reduce the heat, cover the pan and simmer gently for 5 minutes.

3) Remove the pan from the heat and let the sauce cool slightly before puréeing it in a blender.

4) Add the remaining ingredients and blend everything together well. Then serve at room temperature.

spinach and Coconut Sauce

Serves 4

Delicious served cold, try this sauce with Tarka Rice and Paneer Bhujia (pages 132 and 77). The combination is sensational. If you feel like spending more than 30 minutes in the kitchen, you could serve Bread Pakoras or Eggplant Fritters (pages 19 and 13) instead of Paneer Bhujia.

4 cups chopped fresh spinach leaves	1¼ cups hot water
⅔ cup shredded coconut	1 teaspoon salt, or to taste
2 green chilies, seeded and chopped	½ cup whole milk plain yogurt
2 teaspoons peeled and chopped gingerroot	1 tablespoon lime juice

1) Put the spinach, coconut, chilies and ginger into a saucepan and add the hot water. Bring to a boil, then reduce the heat, cover and simmer gently for 10 minutes.

2) Remove the pan from the heat and let the mixture cool slightly.

3) Pour the spinach mixture into a blender and blend until it is smooth, then add the salt, yogurt and lime juice. Blend for a few seconds, then transfer the sauce to a serving dish and serve at room temperature.

Pear and Cucumber Salad

Serves 4

1½ teaspoons cumin seeds

3 firm, ripe Williams or
    Packham pears

1 tablespoon lime juice

1 small or ½ large cucumber

⅔ cup sour cream

½ teaspoon salt

1 teaspoon sugar

½ teaspoon chili powder

1) Heat a small, heavy-based pan over a medium heat. Add the cumin seeds and dry roast them until they are a shade darker and they give up their aroma. Transfer the roasted seeds to a plate and allow them to cool.

2) Peel and core the pears and cut the flesh into bite-sized pieces. Put the pieces into a mixing bowl and sprinkle the lime juice over them.

3) Chop the cucumber into bite-sized pieces to match the pieces of pear and mix them together.

4) Crush the roasted cumin seeds with a pestle or the back of a wooden spoon.

5) Mix the sour cream with the salt, sugar, half the chili powder and half the crushed cumin seeds.

6) Add this mixture to the pear and cucumber pieces and mix everything together well.

7) Transfer the salad to a serving dish and sprinkle the remaining chili powder and crushed cumin seeds over the top. Serve immediately.

Exotic Fruit Salad

Serves 4

1 large, ripe fresh mango
1 small, ripe papaya
15-oz can lychees, drained
15-oz can pineapple cubes,
  drained
1 cup crème fraîche

finely grated zest of 1 orange
2 tablespoons confectioner's
  sugar
2 tablespoons Cointreau
1 tablespoon orange juice

1) Peel the mango and slice as much flesh off from either side of the pit as you can. Chop the flesh into bite-sized pieces.
2) Cut the papaya in half lengthwise and remove the black seeds and the white membrane you will find under the seeds. Peel and chop the papaya flesh into bite-sized pieces.
3) Arrange the fruits in layers in 4 individual glass serving dishes or stemmed glasses.
4) In a bowl, mix the crème fraîche with the remaining ingredients and top each serving of fruit with a helping of the mixture. Serve chilled if desired.

Summer Fruits with Rose-Flavored Cream

Serves 4

*U*se any combination of summer fruits you like. The ones I have used here just happen to be my favorites!

Rooh Afza is a delicious rose-flavored syrup that is great for flavoring cream, ice-cream, fromage frais (fromage blanc) and so on. It also makes a delicious summer drink. All you need to do is dilute it to suit your taste. It is known as the summer drink of the East. All Indian stores sell Rooh Afza.

1 cup pitted and sliced peaches	1¼ cups heavy cream
1 cup blackberries	5 tablespoons rose syrup (Rooh Afza)
1 cup strawberries	
1 cup red currants	4–6 Amaretti biscuits, optional

1) Arrange the fruits in individual serving dishes.
2) Beat the cream and rose syrup together until the cream is thick, but not stiff.
3) Pile the cream on top of the fruits.
4) If using, crush the Amaretti biscuits lightly and sprinkle on top of the cream. Serve immediately.

Summer Fruit Platter with Yogurt Dips

Serves 4

*T*hese yogurt dips taste sensational with summer fruits. You can use plain fromage frais instead of yogurt if you wish.

1½ cups plain yogurt
2 tablespoons rose syrup (Rooh Afza)
¼ cup ready-to-use chocolate sauce

3 cups mixed summer fruits, such as strawberries, raspberries, peaches, mangoes

1) Put half the yogurt in a mixing bowl and the remainder in another mixing bowl.
2) Add the rose syrup to one bowl and the chocolate sauce to the other. Beat each bowlful with a fork until the mixtures are smooth and well blended.
3) Transfer the dips to small serving bowls and chill.
4) Arrange the fruits on a large platter, place the dips in the center and serve.

Spiced Oranges with Grenadine

Serves 4

*F*resh oranges with grenadine look fabulous and taste rather special. You can use canned mandarins to save time, but you will need to drain them. Save a little of the syrup to use as suggested for the fresh oranges here.

8–10 large oranges, such as
    navel
1 teaspoon ground cinnamon

2½ tablespoons grenadine
sliced kiwi fruits, to decorate,
    optional

1) Peel the oranges. Using a small, sharp knife, segment the oranges by cutting down each side of where the orange segments meet, removing the white pith and leaving the membrane behind. Put the segments into a bowl.

2) Sprinkle the cinnamon over the orange segments and mix them together well.

3) Spoon the grenadine into 4 glass serving bowls or stemmed glasses. Lift the orange segments with a slotted spoon and pile them on top of the grenadine, then carefully spoon the juice left behind over each serving.

4) Decorate each serving with the slices of kiwi fruit, if using, and serve.

Mango Dessert

Serves 4

two 15-oz cans mangoes
1 cup cottage cheese
1½ tablespoons granulated
  sugar, or to taste

2 tablespoons rose water
15-oz can lychees, drained
¼ teaspoon ground cardamom
  or nutmeg

1) Purée the mangoes together with their syrup.
2) Add the cottage cheese, sugar and rose water. Mix until well blended.
3) Spoon the mixture into individual serving dishes and top with the lychees.
4) Sprinkle the ground cardamom or nutmeg over each serving and chill for 30 minutes, if you can.

Index